BULLETS & BILLETS

TO MY OLD PALS,
"BILL," "BERT," AND "ALF,"
WHO HAVE SAT IN THE MUD WITH ME

CONTENTS

LIST OF ILLUSTRATIONS

"Bruce Bairnsfather: a photograph"

"The Birth of "Fragments": Scribbles on the farmhouse walls"

That Astronomical Annoyance, the Star Shell, Which Momentarily
Enables You to Scrutinize the Kind of Mud You Are In

An Impression of the Famous Bois de Ploegsteet

"A Hopeless Dawn: Rain, Mud, Damp Coke, and Dug-Out Off Down Stream"

"The usual line in Billeting Farms: A Three-Sided Red-Tiled Building, With a Rectangular Smell in the Middle"

"Chuck us the biscuits, Bill. The fire wants mendin'"

"Shut that blinkin' door. There's a 'ell of a draught in 'ere"

"A Memory of Christmas, 1914: 'Look at this bloke's buttons, 'Arry. I should reckon 'e 'as a maid to dress 'im.'"

What He Doesn't Know About Fire Buckets and the Time the
Rum Comes Up Isn't Worth Knowing

A Messines Memory: "'Ow about shiftin' a bit further down
the road, Fred?"

"Old soldiers never die"

Photograph of the Author. St. Yvon, Christmas Day, 1914
Officers, 2nd Lieutenant: 1
Bairnsfathers, Bruce: 1
Holes, Shell: 1

Off "in" again

"Poor old Maggie! She seems to be 'avin' it dreadful wet at 'ome!"

The Tin-opener

Subterranean Voice, Commenting on the Abnormal Activity of the
Mortar Across the Way: "They're devils to snipe, ain't they, Bill?"

First Discovered in the Alluvial Deposits of Southern Flanders.
Feeds Almost Exclusively on Jam and Water Biscuits.
Hobby: Filling Sandbags, on Dark and Rainy Nights

FOREWORD

Down South, in the Valley of the Somme, far from the spots recorded in this book, I began to write this story.

In billets it was. I strolled across the old farmyard and into the wood beyond. Sitting by a gurgling little stream, I began, with the aid of a notebook and a pencil, to record the joys and sorrows of my first six months in France.

I do not claim any unique quality for these experiences. Many thousands have had the same. I have merely, by request, made a record of my times out there, in the way that they appeared to me.

BRUCE BAIRNSFATHER.

CHAPTER I

LANDING AT HAVRE—TORTONI'S—
FOLLOW THE TRAM LINES—ORDERS
FOR THE FRONT

Gliding up the Seine, on a transport crammed to the lid with troops, in the still, cold hours of a November morning, was my debut into the war. It was about 6 a.m. when our boat silently slipped along past the great wooden sheds, posts and complications of Havre Harbour. I had spent most of the twelve-hour trip down somewhere in the depths of the ship, dealing out rations to the hundred men that I had brought with me from Plymouth. This sounds a comparatively simple process, but not a bit of it. To begin with, the ship was filled with troops to bursting point, and the mere matter of proceeding from one deck to another was about as difficult as trying to get round to see a friend at the other side of the ground at a Crystal Palace Cup final.

I stood in a queue of Gordons, Seaforths, Worcesters, etc., slowly moving up one, until, finally arriving at the companion (nearly said staircase), I tobogganed down into the hold, and spent what was left of the night dealing out those rations. Having finished at last, I came to the surface again, and now, as the transport glided along through the dirty waters of the river, and as I gazed at the motley collection of Frenchmen on the various wharves, and saw a variety of soldiery, and a host of other warlike "props," I felt acutely that now I was *in* the war at last—the real thing! For some time I had been rehearsing in England; but that was over now, and here I was—in the common or garden vernacular—"in the soup."

At last we were alongside, and in due course I had collected that hundred men of mine, and found that the number was still a hundred, after which I landed with the rest, received instructions and a guide, then started off for the Base Camps.

These Camps were about three miles out of Havre, and thither the whole contents of the ship marched in one long column, accompanied on either side by a crowd of ragged little boys shouting for souvenirs and biscuits. I and my hundred men were near the rear of the procession, and in about an hour's time arrived at the Base Camps.

I don't know that it is possible to construct anything more atrociously hideous or uninteresting than a Base Camp. It consists, in military parlance, of nothing more than:—

    Fields, grassless 1
    Tents, bell   500

" Rations "

In fact, a huge space, once a field, now a bog, on which are perched rows and rows of squalid tents.

I stumbled along over the mud with my troupe, and having found the Adjutant, after a considerable search, thought that my task was over, and that I could slink off into some odd tent or other and get a sleep and a rest. Oh no!—the Adjutant had only expected fifty men, and here was I with a hundred.

Consternation! Two hours' telephoning and intricate back-chat with the Adjutant eventually led to my being ordered to leave the expected fifty and take the others to another Base Camp hard by, and see if they would like to have them there.

The rival Base Camp expressed a willingness to have this other fifty, so at last I had finished, and having found an empty tent, lay down on the ground, with my greatcoat for a pillow and went to sleep.

I awoke at about three in the afternoon, got hold of a bucket of water and proceeded to have a wash. Having shaved, washed, brushed my hair, and had a look at the general effect in the polished back of my cigarette case (all my kit was still at the docks), I emerged from my canvas cave and started off to have a look round.

I soon discovered a small café down the road, and found it was a place used by several of the officers who, like myself, were temporarily dumped at the Camps. I went in and got something to eat. Quite a good little place upstairs there was, where one could get breakfast each morning: just coffee, eggs, and bread sort of thing. By great luck I met a pal of mine here; he had come over in a boat previous to mine, and after we had had a bit of a refresher and a smoke we decided to go off down to Havre and see the sights.

A tram passed along in front of this café, and this we boarded. It took about half an hour getting down to Havre from Bléville where the Camps were, but it was worth it.

Tortoni's Café, a place that we looked upon as the last link with civilization: Tortoni's, with its blaze of light, looking-glass and gold paint—its popping corks and hurrying waiters—made a deep and pleasant indent on one's mind, for "to-morrow" meant "the Front" for most of those who sat there.

As we sat in the midst of that kaleidoscopic picture, formed of French, Belgian and English uniforms, intermingled with the varied and gaudy robes of the local nymphs; as we mused in the midst of dense clouds of tobacco smoke, we could not help reflecting that this *might* be the last time we should look on such scenes of revelry, and came to the conclusion that the only thing to do was to make the most of it while we had the chance. And, by Gad, we did . . .

A little after midnight I parted from my companion and started off to get back to that Base Camp of mine.

Standing in the main square of the town, I realized a few points which tended to take the edge off the success of the evening:

No. 1.—It was too late to get a tram.

No. 2.—All the taxis had disappeared.

No. 3.—It was pouring with rain.

No. 4.—I had three miles to go.

I started off to walk it—but had I known what that walk was going to be, I would have buttoned myself round a lamp-post and stayed where I was.

I made that fatal mistake of thinking that I knew the way.

Leaning at an angle of forty-five degrees against the driving rain, I staggered along the tram lines past the Casino, and feeling convinced that the tram lines must be correct, determined to follow them.

After about half an hour's walk, mostly uphill, I became rather suspicious as to the road being quite right.

Seeing a sentry-box outside a palatial edifice on the right, I tacked across the road and looked for the sentry.

A lurid thing in gendarmes advanced upon me, and I let off one of my curtailed French sentences at him:

"Pour Bléville, Monsieur?"

I can't give his answer in French, but being interpreted I think it meant that I was completely on the wrong road, and that he wasn't certain as to how I could ever get back on it without returning to Havre and starting again.

He produced an envelope, made an unintelligible sketch on the back of it, and started me off again down the way I had come.

I realized what my mistake had been. There was evidently a branch tram line, which I had followed, and this I thought could only have branched off near the Casino, so back I went to the Casino and started again.

I was right about the branch line, and started merrily off again, taking as I thought the main line to Bléville.

After another half-hour of this, with eyes feverishly searching for recognizable landmarks, I again began to have doubts as to the veracity of the tram lines. However, pretending that I placed their honesty beyond all doubt, I plodded on; but round a corner, found the outlook so unfamiliar that I determined to ask again. Not a soul about. Presently I discovered a small house, standing back off the road and showing a thin slit of light above the shutters of a downstairs window. I tapped on the glass. A sound as of someone hurriedly trying to hide a pile of coverless umbrellas in a cupboard was followed by the opening of the window, and a bristling head was silhouetted against the light.

I squeezed out the same old sentence:

"Pour Bléville, Monsieur?"

A fearful cataract of unintelligible words burst from the head, but left me almost as much in the dark as ever, though with a faint glimmering that I was "warmer." I felt that if I went back about a mile and turned to the left, all would be well.

I thanked the gollywog in the window, who, somehow or other, I think must have been a printer working late, and started off once more.

After another hour's route march I came to some scattered houses, and finally to a village. I was indignantly staring at a house when suddenly, joy!—I realized that what I was looking at was an unfamiliar view of the café where I had breakfasted earlier in the day.

Another ten minutes and I reached the Camp. Time now 2.30 a.m. I thought I would just take a look in at the Orderly Room tent to see if there were any orders in for me. It was lucky I did. Inside I found an orderly asleep in a blanket, and woke him.

"Anything in for me?" I asked. "Bairnsfather's my name."

"Yes, sir, there is," came through the blanket, and getting up he went to the table at the other end of the tent. He sleepily handed me the wire: "Lieutenant Bairnsfather to proceed to join his battalion as machine-gun officer . . ."

"What time do I have to push off?" I inquired.

"By the eight o'clock from Havre to-morrow, sir."

Time now 3 a.m. To-morrow—THE FRONT! And then I crept into my tent and tried to sleep.

CHAPTER II

TORTUOUS TRAVELLING—CLIPPERS AND TABLETS—DUMPED AT A SIDING— I JOIN MY BATTALION

Not much sleep that night, a sort of feverish coma instead: wild dreams in which I and the gendarme were attacking a German trench, the officer in charge of which we found to be the Base Camp Adjutant after all.

However, I got up early—packed my few belongings in my valise, which had mysteriously turned up from the docks, and went off on the tram down to Havre. That hundred men I had brought over had nothing to do with me now. I was entirely on my own, and was off to the Front to join my battalion. Down at Havre the officials at the station gave me a complicated yellow diagram, known as a travelling pass, and I got into a carriage in the train bound for Rouen.

I was not alone now; a whole forest of second lieutenants like myself were in the same train, and with them a solid, congealed mass of valises, packs, revolvers and haversacks. At last the train started, and after the usual hour spent in feeling that you have left all the most important things behind, I settled down on a mound of equipment and tried to do a bit of a sleep.

So what with sleeping, smoking and talking, we jolted along until we pulled up at Rouen. Here I had to leave the train, for some obscure reason, in order to go to the Palais de Justice to get another ticket. I padded off down over the bridge into Rouen, found the Palais, went in and was shown along to an office that dealt in tickets.

In this dark and dingy oak-panelled saloon, illuminated by electric light and the glittering reflections from gold braid, there lurked a general or two. I was here given another pass entitling me to be deposited at a certain siding in Flanders.

Back I went to the station, and in due course rattled off in the train again towards the North.

A fearfully long journey we had, up to the Front! The worst of it was that nobody knew—or, if they did, wouldn't tell you—which way you were going, or how long it would take to get to your destination. For instance, we didn't know we were going to Rouen till we got there; and we didn't know we were going from Rouen to Boulogne until, after a night spent in the train, the whole outfit jolted and jangled into the Gare de Something, down by the wharf at that salubrious seaport.

We spent a complete day and part of an evening at Boulogne, as our train did not leave until midnight.

I and another chap who was going to the next railhead to mine at the Front, went off together into the town and had lunch at a café in the High Street. We then strolled around the shops, buying a few things we needed. Not very attractive things either, but I'll mention them here to show how we thought and felt.

We first went to a "pharmacie" and got some boxes of morphia tablets, after which we went to an ironmonger's (don't know the French for it) and each bought a ponderous pair of barbed wire cutters. So what with wire clippers and morphia tablets, we *were* gay. About four o'clock we calmed down a bit, and went to the same restaurant where we had lunched.

Here we had tea with a couple of French girls, exceeding good to look upon, who had apparently escaped from Lille. We got on splendidly with them till a couple of French officers, one with the Legion of Honour, came along to the next table. That took all the shine out of us, so we determined to quit, and cleared off to the Hotel de Folkestone, where we had a bath to console us. Dinner followed, and then, feeling particularly hilarious, I made my will. Not the approved will of family lawyer style, but just a letter announcing, in bald and harsh terms that, in the event of my remaining permanently in Belgium, I wanted my total small worldly wealth to be disposed of in a certain way.

Felt better after this outburst, and, rejoining my pal, we went off into the town again and by easy stages reached the train.

At about one a.m. the train started, and we creaked and groaned our way out of Boulogne. We were now really off for the Front, and the situation, consequently, became more exciting. We were slowly getting nearer and nearer to the real thing. But what a train! It dribbled and rumbled along at about five miles an hour, and, I verily believe, stopped at every farmhouse within sight of the line. I could not help thinking that the engine driver was a German in disguise, who was trying to prevent our ever arriving at our destination. I tried to sleep, but each time the train pulled up, I woke with a start and thought that we'd got there. This went on for many hours, and as I knew we must be getting somewhere near, my dreams became worse and worse.

I somehow began to think that the engine driver was becoming cautious—(he was a Frenchman again)—thought that, perhaps, he had to get down occasionally and walk ahead a bit to see if it was safe to go on.

Nobody in the train had the least idea where the Front was, how far off, or what it was like. For all we knew, our train might be going right up into the rear of the front line trenches. Somewhere round 6 a.m. I reached my siding. All the others, except myself and one other, had got out at previous halts. I got down from the carriage on to the cinder track, and went along the line to the station. Nobody about except a few Frenchmen, so I went back to the carriage again, and sat looking out through the dimmed window at the rain-soaked flat country. The other fellow with me was doing the same. A sudden, profound depression came over me. Here was I and this other cove dumped down at this horrible siding; nothing to eat, and nobody to meet us. How rude and callous of someone, or something. I looked at my watch; it had stopped, and on trying to wind it I found it was broken.

I stared out of the window again; gave that up, and stared at the opposite seat. Suddenly my eye caught something shiny under the seat. I stooped and picked it up; it was a watch! I have always looked upon this episode as an omen of some sort; but of what sort I can't quite make out. Finding a watch means finding "Time"—perhaps it meant I would find time to write this book; on the other hand it may have meant that my time had come—who knows?

At about eight o'clock by my new watch I again made an attack on the station, and at last found the R.T.O., which, being interpreted, means the Railway Transport Officer. He told me where my battalion was to be found; but didn't know whether they were in the trenches or out. He also added that if he were me he wouldn't hurry about going there, as I could probably get a lift in an A.S.C. wagon later on. I took his advice, and having left all my tackle by his office, went into the nearest estaminet to get some breakfast. The owner, a genial but garrulous little Frenchman, spent quite a lot of time explaining to me how those hateful people, the Boches, had occupied his house not so long before, and had punched a hole in his kitchen wall to use a machine-gun through. After breakfast I went to the station and arranged for my baggage to be sent on by an A.S.C. wagon, and then started out to walk to Nieppe, which I learnt was the place where my battalion billeted. As I plodded along the muddy road in the pouring rain, I became aware of a sound with which I was afterwards to become horribly familiar.

"Boom!" That was all; but I knew it was the voice of the guns, and in that moment I realized that here was the war, and that I was in it.

I ploughed along for about four miles down uninteresting mud canals—known on maps as roads—until, finally, I entered Nieppe.

The battalion, I heard from a passing soldier, was having its last day in billets prior to going into the trenches again. They were billeted at a disused brewery at the other end of the town. I went on down the squalid street and finally found the place.

A crowd of dirty, war-worn looking soldiers were clustered about the entrance in groups. I went in through the large archway past them into the brewery yard. Soldiers everywhere, resting, talking and smoking. I inquired where the officers' quarters were, and was shown to the brewery head office. Here I found the battalion officers, many of whom I knew, and went into their improvised messroom, which, in previous days, had apparently been the Brewery Board room.

I found everything very dark, dingy and depressing. That night the battalion was going into the trenches again, and last evenings in billets are not generally very exhilarating. I sat and talked with those I knew, and presently the Colonel came in, and I heard what the orders were for the evening. I felt very strange and foreign to it all, as everyone except myself had had their baptism of trench life, and, consequently, at this time I did not possess that calm indifference, bred of painful experience, which is part of the essence of a true trench-dweller.

The evening drew on. We had our last meal in billets—sardines, bread, butter and cake sort of thing—slung on to the bare table by the soldier servants, who were more engrossed in packing up things they were taking to the trenches than in anything else.

And now the time came to start off. I found the machine-gun section in charge of a sergeant, a most excellent fellow, who had looked after the section since the officer (whose place I had come to fill) had been wounded. I took over from him, and, as the battalion moved off along the road, fell in behind with my latest acquisition—a machine-gun section, with machine guns to match. It was quite dusk now, and as we neared the great Bois de Ploegstert, known all over the world as "Plugstreet Wood," it was nearly night. The road was getting rougher, and the houses, dotted about in dark silhouettes against the sky-line, had a curiously deserted and worn appearance. Everything was looking dark, damp and drear.

On we went down the road through the wood, stumbling along in the darkness over the shell-pitted track. Weird noises occasionally floated through the trees; the faint "crack" of a rifle, or the rumble of limber wheels. A distant light flickered momentarily in the air, cutting out in bold relief the ruins of the shattered chateau on our left. On we went through this scene of dark and humid desolation, past the occasional mounds of former habitations, on into the trenches before Plugstreet Wood.

CHAPTER III

THOSE PLUGSTREET TRENCHES—
MUD AND RAIN—FLOODED OUT—
A HOPELESS DAWN

An extraordinary sensation—the first time of going into trenches. The first idea that struck me about them was their haphazard design. There was, no doubt, some very excellent reason for someone or other making those trenches as they were; but they really did strike me as curious when I first saw them.

A trench will, perhaps, run diagonally across a field, will then go along a hedge at right angles, suddenly give it up and start again fifty yards to the left, in such a position that it is bound to cross the kitchen-garden of a shattered chateau, go through the greenhouse and out into the road. On getting there it henceforth rivals the ditch at the side in the amount of water it can run off into a row of dug-outs in the next field. There is, apparently, no necessity for a trench to be in any way parallel to the line of your enemy; as long as he can't shoot you from immediately behind, that's all you ask.

It was a long and weary night, that first one of mine in the trenches. Everything was strange, and wet and horrid. First of all I had to go and fix up my machine guns at various points, and find places for the gunners to sleep in. This was no easy matter, as many of the dug-outs had fallen in and floated off down stream.

In this, and subsequent descriptions of the trenches, I may lay myself open to the charge of exaggeration. But it must be remembered that I am describing trench life in the early days of 1914, and I feel sure that those who had experience of them will acquit me of any such charge.

To give a recipe for getting a rough idea, in case you want to, I recommend the following procedure. Select a flat ten-acre ploughed field, so sited that all the surface water of the surrounding country drains into it. Now cut a zig-zag slot about four feet deep and three feet wide diagonally across, dam off as much water as you can so as to leave about a hundred yards of squelchy mud; delve out a hole at one side of the slot, then endeavour to live there for a month on bully beef and damp biscuits, whilst a friend has instructions to fire at you with his Winchester every time you put your head above the surface.

Well, here I was, anyway, and the next thing was to make the best of it. As I have before said, these were the days of the earliest trenches in this war: days when we had none of those desirable "props," such as corrugated iron, floorboards, and sand bags *ad lib*.

" 'ullo ! 'Arry

When you made a dug-out in those days you made it out of anything you could find, and generally had to make it yourself. That first night I was "in" I discovered, after a humid hour or so, that our battalion wouldn't fit into the spaces left by the last one, and as regards dug-outs, the truth of that mathematical axiom, "Two's into one, won't go," suddenly dawned on me with painful clearness. I was faced with making a dug-out, and it was raining, of course. (*Note.*—Whenever I don't state the climatic conditions, read "raining.") After sloshing about in several primitive trenches in the vicinity of the spot where we had fixed our best machine-gun position, my sergeant and I discovered a sort of covered passage in a ditch in front of a communication trench. It was a sort of emergency exit back from a row of ramshackle, water-logged hovels in the ditch to the communication trench. We decided to make use of this passage, and arranged things in such a way that by scooping out the clay walls we made two caves, one behind the other. The front one was about five yards from the machine gun, and you reached the back cave by going through the outer one. It now being about 11 p.m., and having been for the last five hours perpetually on the scramble, through trenches of all sorts, I drew myself into the inner cave to go to sleep.

This little place was about 4 feet long, 3 feet high, and 3 feet wide. I got out my knife, took a scoop out of the clay wall, and fishing out a candle-end from my pocket, stuck it in the niche, lit it and a cigarette. I now lay down and tried to size up the situation and life in general.

Here I was, in this horrible clay cavity, somewhere in Belgium, miles and miles from home. Cold, wet through and covered with mud. This was the first day; and, so far as I could see, the future contained nothing but repetitions of the same thing, or worse.

Nothing was to be heard except the occasional crack of the sniper's shot, the dripping of the rain, and the low murmur of voices from the outer cave.

In the narrow space beside me lay my equipment; revolver, and a sodden packet of cigarettes. Everything damp, cold and dark; candle-end guttering. I think suddenly of something like the Empire or the Alhambra, or anything else that's reminiscent of brightness and life, and then—swish, bang—back to the reality that the damp clay wall is only eighteen inches in front of me; that here I am—that the Boche is just on the other side of the field; and that there doesn't seem the slightest chance of leaving except in an ambulance.

My machine-gun section for the gun near by lay in the front cave, a couple of feet from me; their spasmodic talking gradually died away as, one by one, they dropped off to sleep. One more indignant, hopeless glare at the flickering candle-end, then I pinched the wick, curled up, and went to sleep.

* * * * *

A sudden cold sort of peppermint sensation assailed me; I awoke and sat up. My head cannoned off the clay ceiling, so I partially had to lie down again.

I attempted to strike a match, but found the whole box was damp and sodden. I heard a muttering of voices and a curse or two in the outer cavern, and presently the sergeant entered my sanctum on all fours:

"We're bein' flooded out, sir; there's water a foot deep in this place of ours."

That explains it. I feel all round the back of my greatcoat and find I have been sleeping in a pool of water.

I crawled out of my inner chamber, and the whole lot of us dived through the rapidly rising water into the ditch outside. I scrambled up on to the top of the bank, and tried to focus the situation.

From inquiries and personal observation I found that the cause of the tide rising was the fact that the Engineers had been draining the trench, in the course of which process they had apparently struck a spring of water.

We accepted the cause of the disaster philosophically, and immediately discussed what was the best thing to be done. Action of some sort was urgently necessary, as at present we were all sitting on the top of the mud bank of the ditch in the silent, steady rain, the whole party being occasionally illuminated by a German star shell—more like a family sitting for a flashlight photograph than anything else.

We decided to make a dam. Having found an empty ration box and half a bag of coke, we started on the job of trying to fence off the water from our cave. After about an hour's struggle with the elements we at last succeeded, with the aid of the ration box, the sack of coke and a few tins of bully, in reducing the water level inside to six inches.

Here we were, now wetter than ever, cold as Polar bears, sitting in this hygroscopic catacomb at about 2 a.m. We longed for a fire; a fire was decided on. We had a fire bucket—it had started life as a biscuit tin—a few bits of damp wood, but no coke. "We had some coke, I'm sure! Why, of course—we built it into the dam!" Down came the dam, out came the coke, and in came the water. However, we preferred the water to the cold; so, finally, after many exasperating efforts, we got a fire going in the bucket. Five minutes' bliss followed by disaster. The fire bucket proceeded to emit such dense volumes of sulphurous smoke that in a few moments we couldn't see a lighted match.

We stuck it a short time longer, then one by one dived into the water and out into the air, shooting out of our mud hovel to the surface like snakes when you pour water down their holes.

Time now 3 a.m. No sleep; rain, water, *plus* smoke. A board meeting held immediately decides to give up sleep and dug-outs for that night. A motion to try and construct a chimney with an entrenching tool is defeated by five votes to one . . . dawn is breaking—my first night in trenches comes to an end.

CHAPTER IV

MORE MUD—RAIN AND BULLETS—
A BIT OF CAKE—"WIND UP"—
NIGHT ROUNDS

The rose-pink sky fades off above to blue,
    The morning star alone proclaims the dawn.
The empty tins and barbed wire bathed in dew
    Emerge, and then another day is born.

I wrote that "poem" in those—trenches, so you can see the sort of state to which I was reduced.

Well, my first trench night was over; the dawn had broken—everything else left to break had been seen to by the artillery, which started off generally at about eight. And what a fearful long day it seemed, that first one! As soon as it was light I began scrambling about, and having a good look at the general lie of things. In front was a large expanse of root field, at the further side of which a long irregular parapet marked the German trenches. Behind those again was more root field, dented here and there with shell holes filled with water, beyond which stood a few isolated remnants which had once been cottages. I stood at a projection in one of our trenches, from where I could see the general shape of our line, and could glimpse a good view of the German arrangements. Not a soul could be seen anywhere. Here and there a wisp of smoke indicated a fire bucket. Behind our trenches, behind the shattered houses at the top of a wooded rise in the ground, stood what once must have been a fine chateau. As I looked, a shrieking hollow whistle overhead, a momentary pause, then—"Crumph!" showed clearly what was the matter with the chateau. It was being shelled. The Germans seemed to have a rooted objection to that chateau. Every morning, as we crouched in our mud kennels, we heard those "Crumphs," and soon got to be very good judges of form. *We* knew they were shelling the chateau. When they didn't shell the chateau, we got it in the trenches; so we looked on that dear old mangled wreck with a friendly eye—that tapering, twisted, perforated spire, which they never could knock down, was an everlasting bait to the Boche, and a perfect fairy godmother to us.

Oh, those days in that trench of ours! Each day seemed about a week long. I shared a dug-out with a platoon commander after that first night. The machine-gun section found a suitable place and made a dug-out for themselves.

Day after day, night after night, my companion and I lay and listened to the daily explosions, read, and talked, and sloshed about that trench together.

The greatest interest one had in the daytime was sitting on the damp straw in our clay vault, scraping the mud off one's saturated boots and clothes. The event to which one looked forward with the greatest interest was the arrival of letters in the evening.

Now and again we got out of our dug-out and sloshed down the trench to scheme out some improvement or other, or to furtively look out across the water-logged turnip field at the Boche trenches opposite. Occasionally, in the silent, still, foggy mornings, a voice from somewhere in the alluvial depths of a miserable trench, would suddenly burst into a scrap of song, such as—

Old soldiers never die,
     They simply fade away.

—a voice full of "fed-upness," steeped in determination.

Then all would be silence for the next couple of hours, and so the day passed.

"The Knave of Spades".

At dusk, my job was to emerge from this horrible drain and go round the various machine-gun positions. What a job! I generally went alone, and in the darkness struck out across the sodden field, tripping, stumbling, and sometimes falling into various shell holes on the way.

One does a little calling at this time of day. Having seen a gun in another trench, one looks up the nearest platoon commander. You look into so-and-so's dug-out and find it empty. You ask a sergeant where the occupant is.

"He's down the trench, sir." You push your way down the trench, dodging pools of water and stepping over fire buckets, mess tins, brushing past men standing, leaning or sitting—right on down the trench, where, round a corner, you find the platoon commander. "Well, if we can't get any sandbags," he is probably saying to a sergeant, "we will just have to bank it up with earth, and put those men on the other side of the traverse," or something like that. He turns to me and says, "Come along back to my dug-out and have a bit of cake. Someone or other has sent one out from home."

We start back along the trench. Suddenly a low murmuring, rattling sound can be heard in the distance. We stop to listen, the sound gets louder; everyone stops to listen—the sound approaches, and is now distinguishable as rifle-fire. The firing becomes faster and faster; then suddenly swells into a roar and now comes the phenomenon of trench warfare: "wind up"—the prairie fire of the trenches.

Everyone stands to the parapet, and away on the left a tornado of crackling sound can be heard, getting louder and louder. In a few seconds it has swept on down the line, and now a deafening rattle of rifle-fire is going on immediately in front. Bullets are flicking the tops of the sandbags on the parapet in hundreds, whilst white streaks are shooting up with a swish into the sky and burst into bright radiating blobs of light—the star shell at its best.

A curious thing, this "wind up." We never knew when it would come on. It is caused entirely by nerves. Perhaps an inquisitive Boche, somewhere a mile or two on the left, had thought he saw someone approaching his barbed wire; a few shots are exchanged—a shout or two, followed by more shots—panic—more shots—panic spreading—then suddenly the whole line of trenches on a front of a couple of miles succumbs to that well-known malady, "wind up."

In reality it is highly probable that there was no one in front near the wire, and no one has had the least intention of being there.

Presently there comes a deep "boom" from somewhere in the distance behind, and a large shell sails over our heads and explodes somewhere amongst the Boches; another and another, and then all becomes quiet again. The rifle fire diminishes and soon ceases. Total result of one of these firework displays: several thousand rounds of ammunition squibbed off, hundreds of star shells wasted, and no casualties.

It put the "wind up" me at first, but I soon got to know these affairs, and learnt to take them calmly.

I went along with the platoon commander back to his lair. An excellent fellow he was. No one in this war could have hated it all more than he did, and no one could have more conscientiously done his very best at it. Poor fellow, he was afterwards killed near Ypres.

"Well, how are things going with you?" I said.

"Oh, all right. They knocked down that same bit of parapet again to-day. I think they must imagine we've got a machine gun there, or something. That's twice we've had to build it up this week. Have a bit of cake?"

So I had a bit of cake and left him; he going back to that old parapet again, whilst I struck off into the dark, wet field towards another gun position, falling into an unfamiliar "Johnson 'ole" on the way.

No one gets a better idea of the general lie of the position than a machine-gun officer. In those early, primitive days, when we had so few of each thing, we, of course, had few machine guns, and these had to be sprinkled about a position to the best possible advantage. The consequence was that people like myself had to cover a considerable amount of ground before our rambles in the dark each night were done.

One machine gun might be, say, in "Dead Man Farm"; another at the "Barrier" near the cross roads; whilst another couple were just at some effective spot in a trench, or in a commanding position in a shattered farm or cottage behind the front line trenches.

I would leave my dug-out as soon as it was dark and do the round of all the guns every night. Just as a sample, I will carry on from where I left the platoon commander.

I slosh across the ploughed field at what I feel to be a correct angle to bring me out on the cross roads, where, about two hundred yards away, I have another gun. I scramble across a broken gateway and an old bit of trench, and close behind come to a deep cutting into which I jump.

About five yards along this I come to a machine-gun emplacement, with a machine-gun sentry on guard.

"Where's the corporal?"

"I'm 'ere, sir," is emitted from the slimy depths of a narrow low-roofed dug-out, and the corporal emerges, hooking back the waterproof sheet as he comes out to prevent the light showing.

"How about this gun, Corporal—is everything all right?"

"Yes, sir; but I was looking around to-day, and thought that if we was to shift the gun over there, where the dead cow is, we'd get a better field of fire."

Meeting adjourned to inspect this valuable site from the windward side.

After a short, blood-thirsty conversation relative to the perforating of the enemy, I leave and push off into the bog again, striking out for another visit. Finally, after two hours' visiting, floundering, bullet dodging, and star shell shirking, accompanied by a liberal allowance of "narrow squeaks," I get back to my own bit of trench; and tobogganing down where I erroneously think the clay steps are, I at last reach my dug-out, and entering on all fours, crouch amongst the damp tobacco leaves and straw and light a cigarette.

CHAPTER V

MY MAN FRIDAY—"CHUCK US THE BISCUITS"—RELIEVED—BILLETS

It was during this first time up in the trenches that I got a soldier servant.

As I had arrived only just in time to go with the battalion to the trenches, the acquisition had to be made by a search in the mud. I found a fellow who hadn't been an officer's servant before, but who wanted to be. I liked the look of him; so feeling rather like Robinson Crusoe, when he booked up Friday, "I got me a man."

He lived in a dug-out about five yards away, and from then onwards continued with me right to the point where this book finishes. This fellow of mine did all my cooking, such as it was, and worked in conjunction with my friend, the platoon commander's servant. Cooking, at the times I write about, consisted of making innumerable brews of tea, and opening tins of bully and Maconochie. Occasionally bacon had to be fried in a mess-tin lid. One day my man soared off into culinary fancies and curried a Maconochie. I have never quite forgiven him for this; I am nearly right again now.

These two soldier servants never had to leave the trench. It was their job to try and find something to make a fire with, and to do all they could to keep the water out of our dug-out, a task which not one of us succeeded in doing. My plan for sustaining life under these conditions was to change my boots as often as possible. If there wasn't time for this I used to try and boil the water in my boots by keeping my feet to the fire bucket. I always put my puttees on first and then a pair of thick socks, and finally a pair of boots. I could, by this means, hurriedly slip off the sodden pair of boots and socks and slip on another set which had become fairly dry by the fire. We lived perpetually damp, if not thoroughly wet. My puttees, which I rarely removed, were more like long rolls of the consistency of nougat than anything else, thanks to the mud. Dug-outs had no wooden linings in those days; no corrugated iron roofs; no floorboards. They were just holes in the clay side of the fire trench, with any old thing for a roof, and old straw or tobacco leaves, which we pinched from some abandoned farm, for a floor. So, you see, there was not much of a chance of dodging the moisture.

The cold was what got me. Personally, I would far rather have gone without food than a fire. A fire of some sort was the only thing to cheer. Coke was scarce and always wet, and it was by no means uncommon to over-hear a remark of this sort: "Chuck us the biscuits, Bill; the fire wants mendin'."

At night I would frequently sally forth to a cracked up village behind, and perhaps procure half a mantelpiece and an old clog to stoke our "furnace" with.

Well, after the usual number of long days and still longer nights spent under these conditions, we came to the day when it was our turn to go out to rest billets, and a relieving battalion to come in. What a splendid day that is! You start "packing" at about 4 p.m. As soon as it is dusk the servants slink off across that turnip morass behind and drag our few belongings back to where the limbers are. These limbers have come up from about three to four miles away, from the Regimental Transport headquarters, to take all the trench "props" back to the billets.

We don't leave, ourselves, until the "incoming" battalion has taken over.

After what seems an interminable wait, we hear a clinking of mess tins and rattling of equipment, the sloshing of feet in the mud, and much whispered profanity, which all goes to announce to you that "they're here!" Then you know that the other battalion has arrived, and are now about to take over these precious slots in the ground.

When the exchange is complete, we are free to go!—to go out for our few days in billets!

The actual going out and getting clear of the trenches takes a long time. Handing over, and finally extricating ourselves from the morass, in the dark, with all our belongings, is a lengthy process; and then we have about a mile of country which we have never been able to examine in the day time, and get familiar with, to negotiate. This is before we get to the high road, and really start for billets.

I had the different machine-gun sections to collect from their various guns, and this not until the relieving sections had all turned up. It was a good two hours' job getting all the sections with their guns, ammunition and various extras finally collected together in the dark a mile back, ready to put all the stuff in the limbers, and so back to billets. When all was fixed up I gave the order and off we started, plodding along back down the narrow, dreary road towards our resting-place. But it was quite a cheerful tramp, knowing as we did that we were going to four days' comparative rest, and, anyway, safety.

On we went down the long, flat, narrow roads, occasionally looking round to see the faint flicker of a star shell showing over the tops of the trees, and to think momentarily of the "poor devils" left behind to take our place, and go on doing just what we had been at. Then, finally, getting far enough away to forget, songs and jokes took us chirping along, past objects which soon became our landmarks in the days to come. On we went, past estaminets, shrines and occasional windmills, down the long winding road for about four miles, until at last we reached our billets, where the battalion willingly halted and dispersed to its various quarters. I and my machine-gun section had still to carry on, for we lived apart, a bit further on, at the Transport Farm. So we continued on our own for another mile and a half, past the estaminet at Romerin, out on towards Neuve Eglise to our Transport Farm. This was the usual red-tiled Belgian farm, with a rectangular smell in the middle.

CHAPTER VI

THE TRANSPORT FARM—FLEECED BY THE FLEMISH—RIDING— NEARING CHRISTMAS

It was about 9 p.m. when we turned into the courtyard of the farm. My sergeant saw to the unlimbering, and dismissed the section, whilst I went into the farm and dismantled myself of all my tackle, such as revolver, field-glass, greatcoat, haversacks, etc.

My servant had, of course, preceded me, and by the time I had made a partial attempt at cleaning myself, he had brought in a meal of sorts and laid it on the oilcloth-covered table by the stove. I was now joined by the transport officer and the regimental quartermaster. They lived at this farm permanently, and only came to the trenches on occasional excursions. They had both had a go at the nasty part of warfare though, before this, so although consumed with a sneaking envy, I was full of respect for them.

We three had a very merry and genial time together. We now had something distinctly resembling a breakfast, a lunch, and a dinner, each day. The transport officer took a lively interest in the efforts of Messrs. Fortnum and Mason, and thus added generously to our menus. It was a glorious feeling, pushing open the door of that farm and coming in from all the wet, darkness, mud and weariness of four days in the trenches. After the supper, I disappeared into the back kitchen place and did what was possible in the shaving and washing line. The Belgian family were all herded away in here, as their front rooms were now our exclusive property. I have never quite made out what the family consisted of, but, approximately, I should think, mother and father and ten children. I am pretty certain about the children, as about half a platoon stood around me whilst shaving, and solemnly watched me with dull brown Flemish eyes. The father kept in the background, resting, I fancy, from his usual day's work of hiding unattractive turnips in enormous numbers, under mounds of mud—(the only form of farming industry which came under my notice in Flanders).

The mother, however, was "all there," in more senses than one. She was of about observation balloon proportions, and had an unerring eye for the main chance. Her telegraphic address, I should imagine, was "Fleecem." She had one sound commercial idea, *i.e.*, "charge as much as you can for everything they want, hide everything they *do* want, and slowly collect any property, in the way of food, they have in the cellar; so that, in the future, there shall be no lack of bully and jam in our farm, at any rate."

They had one farm labourer, a kind of epileptic who, I found out, gave his services in return for being fed—no pay. He will regret this contract of his in time, as the food in question was bully beef and plum and apple jam, with an occasional change to Maconochie and apple and plum jam. That store in the cellar absolutely precludes him from any change from this diet for many years to come. Of course, I must say his work was not such as would be classed amongst the skilled or intellectual trades; it was, apparently, to pump all the accumulated drainage from a subterranean vault out into the yard in front, about twice a week, the rest of his time being taken up by assisting at the hiding of the turnips.

After I had washed and shaved under the critical eyes of Angèle, Rachel, André and Co., I retired into an inner chamber which had once been an apple store, and went to bed on a straw mattress in the corner. Pyjamas at last! and an untroubled sleep. Occasionally in the night one would wake and, listening at the open window, would hear the distant rattle of rifle fire far away beyond the woods.

These four days at the Transport Farm were days of wallowing in rest. There was, of course, certain work to be done in connection with the machine-gun department, such as overhauling and cleaning the guns, and drilling the section at intervals; but the evenings and nights were a perfect joy after those spent in the trenches.

One could walk about the fields near by; could read, write letters, and sleep as much as one liked. And if one wished, walk or ride over to see friends at the other billets. Ah, yes! ride—I am sorry to say that riding was not, and is not, my forte. Unfortunate this, as the machine-gun officer is one of the few privileged to have a horse. I was entitled to ride to the trenches, and ride away from them, and during our rest, ride wherever I wanted to go; but these advantages, so coveted by my horseless pals in the regiment, left me cold. I never will be any good at the "Haute Ecole" act, I'm sure, although I made several attempts to get a liking for the subject in France. When the final day came for our departure to the trenches again, I rode from that Transport Farm.

Riding in England, or in any civilized country, is one thing, and riding in those barren, shell-torn wastes of Flanders is another. The usual darkness, rain and mud pervaded the scene when the evening came for our return journey to the trenches. My groom (curse him) had not forgotten to saddle the horse and bring it round. There it was, standing gaunt and tall in front of the paraded machine-gun section. With my best equestrian demeanour I crossed the yard, and hauling myself up on to my horse, choked out a few commands to the section, and sallied forth on to the road towards the trenches.

Thank Heaven, I didn't go into the Cavalry. The roads about the part we were performing in were about two yards wide and a precipitous ditch at each side. In the middle, all sorts and conditions of holes punctuated their long winding length. Add to this the fact that you are either meeting, or being passed by, a motor lorry every ten minutes, and you will get an idea of the conditions under which riding takes place.

Well, anyway, during the whole of my equestrian career in France, I never came off. I rode along in front of my section, balancing on this "Ship of the Desert" of mine, past all the same landmarks, cracked houses, windmills, estaminets, etc. I experienced innumerable tense moments when my horse—as frequently happened—took me for a bit of a circular tour in an adjacent field, so as to avoid some colossal motor lorry with one headlight of about a million candle-power, which would suddenly roar its way down our single narrow road. At last we got to the dumping-ground spot again—the spot where we horsemen have to come to earth and walk, and where everything is unbaled from the limbers. Here we were again, on the threshold of the trenches.

This monotonous dreary routine of "in" and "out" of the trenches had to be gone through many, many times before we got to Christmas Day. But, during that pre-Christmas period, there was one outstanding feature above the normal dangerous dreariness of the trenches: that was a slight affair in the nature of our attack on the 18th of December, so in the next chapter I will proceed to outline my part in this passage of arms.

CHAPTER VII

A PROJECTED ATTACK—-
DIGGING A SAP—AN 'ELL OF A NIGHT—
THE ATTACK—PUNCTURING PRUSSIANS

One evening I was sitting, coiled up in the slime at the bottom of my dug-out, toying with the mud enveloping my boots, when a head appeared at a gap in my mackintosh doorway and said, "The Colonel wants to see you, sir." So I clambered out and went across the field, down a trench, across a road and down a trench again to where the headquarter dug-outs lay all in a row.

I came to the Colonel's dug-out, where, by the light of a candle-end stuck on an improvised table, he was sitting, busily explaining something by the aid of a map to a group of our officers. I waited till he had finished, knowing that he would want to see me after the others, as the machine-gunner's job is always rather a specialized side-line. Soon he explained to me what he wished me to do with my guns, and gave me a rough outline of the projected attack. He pointed out on the map where he wished me to take up positions, and closed the interview by saying that he thought I should at once proceed to reconnoitre the proposed sites, and lay all my plans for getting into position, as we were going to conduct an operation on the Boches at dawn the next day.

I left, and started at once on my plans. The first thing was to have a thorough good look at the ground, and examine all the possibilities for effective machine-gun co-operation. I determined to take my sergeant along with me, so that he would be as familiar with the scheme in hand as I was. It was raining, of course, and the night was as black as pitch when we both started out on our Sherlock Holmes excursion. I explained the idea of the attack to him, and the part we had to play. The troops on our right were going to carry out the actual attack, and we, on their left flank, were going to lend assistance by engaging the Deutschers in front and by firing half-right to cover our men's advance. My job was clear enough. I had to bring as many machine guns as I could spare down to the right of our own line to assist as much as possible in the real attack. My sergeant and I went down to examine the ground where it was essential for us to fix up. We got to our last trench on the right, and clambering over the parapet, did what we could to find out the nature of the ground in front, and see how we could best fix our machine guns to cover the enemy. We soon saw that in order to get a really clear field of fire it was necessary for us to sap out from the end of our existing right-hand trench and make a machine-gun emplacement at the end.

This necessitated the digging of a sap of about ten yards in length, collecting all the materials for making an emplacement, and mounting our machine gun. It was now about 11 p.m., and all this work had to be completed before dawn.

Having rapidly realized that there was not the slightest prospect of any sleep, and that the morrow looked like being a busy day, we commenced with characteristic fed-up vigour to carry out our nefarious design.

'Ere, you leave that
— rum jar alone"

A section, myself and the sergeant, started on digging that sap, and what a job it was! The Germans were particularly restless that night; kept on squibbing away whilst we were digging, and as it was some time before we had the sap deep enough to be able to stand upright without fear of a puncture in some part of our anatomy, it was altogether most unpleasant. At about an hour before dawn we had got as far as making the emplacement. This we started to put together as hard as we could. We filled sandbags with the earth excavated from the sap, and with frenzied energy tried to complete our defences before dawn. The rain and darkness, both very intense that night, were really very trying. One would pause, shovel in hand, lean against the clay side of the sap, and hurriedly contemplate the scene. Five men, a sergeant and myself, wet through and muddy all over; no sleep, little to eat, silently digging and filling sandbags with an ever-watchful eye for the breaking of the dawn.

Light was breaking across the sky before the job was done, and we had still to complete the top guard of our emplacement. Then we had some fireworks. The nervy Boches had spotted our sap as something new, and their bullets, whacking up against our newly-thrown-up parapet, made us glad we had worked so busily.

We were bound to complete that emplacement, so, at convenient intervals, we crept to the opening, and after saying "one, two, three!" suddenly plumped a newly-filled sandbag on the top. Each time we did this half a dozen bullets went zipping through the canvas or just past overhead. This operation had to be done about a dozen times.

A warm job! At last it was finished, and we sank down into the bottom of the sap to rest. The time for the artillery bombardment had been fixed to begin at about 6 a.m., if I remember rightly, so we got a little rest between finishing our work and the attack itself.

Of course the whole of this enterprise, as far as the bombardment and attack were concerned, cannot be compared with the magnitude of a similar performance in 1915. All the same, it was pretty bad, but not anything like so accurately calculated, or so mechanically efficient as our later efforts in this line. The precise time-table methods of the present period did not exist then, but the main idea of giving the Opposition as much heavy lyddite, followed by shrapnel, was the same.

At about half-past six, as we sat in the sap, we heard the first shell go over. I went to the end of the traverse alongside the emplacement, and watched the German trenches. We were ready to fire at any of the enemy we could see, and when the actual attack started, at the end of the bombardment, we were going to keep up a perpetual sprinkling of bullets along their reserve trenches. A few isolated houses stood just in line with the German trenches. Our gunners had focussed on these, and they gave them a good pasting.

"Crumph! bang! bang! crumph!"—hard at it all the time, whilst shrapnel burst and whizzed about all along the German parapet. The view in front soon became a sort of haze of black dust, as "heavy" after "heavy" burst on top of the Boche positions. Columns of earth and black smoke shot up like giant fountains into the air. I caught sight of a lot of the enemy running along a shallow communication trench of theirs, apparently with the intention of reinforcing their front line. We soon had our machine gun peppering up these unfortunates, and from that moment on kept up an incessant fire on the enemy.

On my left, two of our companies were keeping up a solid rapid fire on the German lines immediately in front.

At last the bombardment ceased. A confused sound of shouts and yells on our right, intermingled with a terrific crackle of rifle fire, told us the attack had started. Without ceasing, we kept up the only assistance we could give: our persistent firing half-right.

How long it all lasted I can't remember; but when I crept into a soldier's dug-out, back in one of our trenches, completely exhausted, I heard that we had taken the enemy trench, but that, unfortunately, owing to its enfiladed position, we had to abandon it later.

Such was my first experience of this see-saw warfare of the trenches.

A few days later, as I happened to be passing through poor, shattered Plugstreet Wood, I came across a clearance 'midst the trees.

Two rows of long, brown mounds of earth, each surmounted by a rough, simple wooden cross, was all that was inside the clearing. I stopped, and looked, and thought—then went away.

CHAPTER VIII

CHRISTMAS EVE—A LULL IN HATE— BRITON CUM BOCHE

Shortly after the doings set forth in the previous chapter we left the trenches for our usual days in billets. It was now nearing Christmas Day, and we knew it would fall to our lot to be back in the trenches again on the 23rd of December, and that we would, in consequence, spend our Christmas there. I remember at the time being very down on my luck about this, as anything in the nature of Christmas Day festivities was obviously knocked on the head. Now, however, looking back on it all, I wouldn't have missed that unique and weird Christmas Day for anything.

Well, as I said before, we went "in" again on the 23rd. The weather had now become very fine and cold. The dawn of the 24th brought a perfectly still, cold, frosty day. The spirit of Christmas began to permeate us all; we tried to plot ways and means of making the next day, Christmas, different in some way to others. Invitations from one dug-out to another for sundry meals were beginning to circulate. Christmas Eve was, in the way of weather, everything that Christmas Eve should be.

I was billed to appear at a dug-out about a quarter of a mile to the left that evening to have rather a special thing in trench dinners—not quite so much bully and Maconochie about as usual. A bottle of red wine and a medley of tinned things from home deputized in their absence. The day had been entirely free from shelling, and somehow we all felt that the Boches, too, wanted to be quiet. There was a kind of an invisible, intangible feeling extending across the frozen swamp between the two lines, which said "This is Christmas Eve for both of us—*something* in common."

About 10 p.m. I made my exit from the convivial dug-out on the left of our line and walked back to my own lair. On arriving at my own bit of trench I found several of the men standing about, and all very cheerful. There was a good bit of singing and talking going on, jokes and jibes on our curious Christmas Eve, as contrasted with any former one, were thick in the air. One of my men turned to me and said:

"You can 'ear 'em quite plain, sir!"

"Hear what?" I inquired.

"The Germans over there, sir; 'ear 'em singin' and playin' on a band or somethin'."

I listened;—away out across the field, among the dark shadows beyond, I could hear the murmur of voices, and an occasional burst of some unintelligible song would come floating out on the frosty air. The singing seemed to be loudest and most distinct a bit to our right. I popped into my dug-out and found the platoon commander.

"Do you hear the Boches kicking up that racket over there?" I said.

"Yes," he replied; "they've been at it some time!"

"Come on," said I, "let's go along the trench to the hedge there on the right—that's the nearest point to them, over there."

So we stumbled along our now hard, frosted ditch, and scrambling up on to the bank above, strode across the field to our next bit of trench on the right. Everyone was listening. An improvised Boche band was playing a precarious version of "Deutschland, Deutschland, uber Alles," at the conclusion of which, some of our mouth-organ experts retaliated with snatches of ragtime songs and imitations of the German tune. Suddenly we heard a confused shouting from the other side. We all stopped to listen. The shout came again. A voice in the darkness shouted in English, with a strong German accent, "Come over here!" A ripple of mirth swept along our trench, followed by a rude outburst of mouth organs and laughter. Presently, in a lull, one of our sergeants repeated the request, "Come over here!"

"You come half-way—I come half-way," floated out of the darkness.

"Come on, then!" shouted the sergeant. "I'm coming along the hedge!"

"Ah! but there are two of you," came back the voice from the other side.

Well, anyway, after much suspicious shouting and jocular derision from both sides, our sergeant went along the hedge which ran at right-angles to the two lines of trenches. He was quickly out of sight; but, as we all listened in breathless silence, we soon heard a spasmodic conversation taking place out there in the darkness.

Presently, the sergeant returned. He had with him a few German cigars and cigarettes which he had exchanged for a couple of Maconochie's and a tin of Capstan, which he had taken with him. The séance was over, but it had given just the requisite touch to our Christmas Eve—something a little human and out of the ordinary routine.

After months of vindictive sniping and shelling, this little episode came as an invigorating tonic, and a welcome relief to the daily monotony of antagonism. It did not lessen our ardour or determination; but just put a little human punctuation mark in our lives of cold and humid hate. Just on the right day, too—Christmas Eve! But, as a curious episode, this was nothing in comparison to our experience on the following day.

On Christmas morning I awoke very early, and emerged from my dug-out into the trench. It was a perfect day. A beautiful, cloudless blue sky. The ground hard and white, fading off towards the wood in a thin low-lying mist. It was such a day as is invariably depicted by artists on Christmas cards—the ideal Christmas Day of fiction.

"Fancy all this hate, war, and discomfort on a day like this!" I thought to myself. The whole spirit of Christmas seemed to be there, so much so that I remember thinking, "This indescribable something in the air, this Peace and Goodwill feeling, surely will have some effect on the situation here to-day!" And I wasn't far wrong; it did around us, anyway, and I have always been so glad to think of my luck in, firstly, being actually in the trenches on Christmas Day, and, secondly, being on the spot where quite a unique little episode took place.

Everything looked merry and bright that morning—the discomforts seemed to be less, somehow; they seemed to have epitomized themselves in intense, frosty cold. It was just the sort of day for Peace to be declared. It would have made such a good finale. I should like to have suddenly heard an immense siren blowing. Everybody to stop and say, "What was that?" Siren blowing again: appearance of a small figure running across the frozen mud waving something. He gets closer—a telegraph boy with a wire! He hands it to me. With trembling fingers I open it: "War off, return home.—George, R.I." Cheers! But no, it was a nice, fine day, that was all.

Walking about the trench a little later, discussing the curious affair of the night before, we suddenly became aware of the fact that we were seeing a lot of evidences of Germans. Heads were bobbing about and showing over their parapet in a most reckless way, and, as we looked, this phenomenon became more and more pronounced.

A complete Boche figure suddenly appeared on the parapet, and looked about itself. This complaint became infectious. It didn't take "Our Bert" long to be up on the skyline (it is one long grind to ever keep him off it). This was the signal for more Boche anatomy to be disclosed, and this was replied to by all our Alf's and Bill's, until, in less time than it takes to tell, half a dozen or so of each of the belligerents were outside their trenches and were advancing towards each other in no-man's land.

A strange sight, truly!

I clambered up and over our parapet, and moved out across the field to look. Clad in a muddy suit of khaki and wearing a sheepskin coat and Balaclava helmet, I joined the throng about half-way across to the German trenches.

It all felt most curious: here were these sausage-eating wretches, who had elected to start this infernal European fracas, and in so doing had brought us all into the same muddy pickle as themselves.

This was my first real sight of them at close quarters. Here they were—the actual, practical soldiers of the German army. There was not an atom of hate on either side that day; and yet, on our side, not for a moment was the will to war and the will to beat them relaxed. It was just like the interval between the rounds in a friendly boxing match. The difference in type between our men and theirs was very marked. There was no contrasting the spirit of the two parties. Our men, in their scratch costumes of dirty, muddy khaki, with their various assorted headdresses of woollen helmets, mufflers and battered hats, were a light-hearted, open, humorous collection as opposed to the sombre demeanour and stolid appearance of the Huns in their grey-green faded uniforms, top boots, and pork-pie hats.

The shortest effect I can give of the impression I had was that our men, superior, broadminded, more frank, and lovable beings, were regarding these faded, unimaginative products of perverted kulture as a set of objectionable but amusing lunatics whose heads had *got* to be eventually smacked.

"Look at that one over there, Bill," our Bert would say, as he pointed out some particularly curious member of the party.

I strolled about amongst them all, and sucked in as many impressions as I could. Two or three of the Boches seemed to be particularly interested in me, and after they had walked round me once or twice with sullen curiosity stamped on their faces, one came up and said "Offizier?" I nodded my head, which means "Yes" in most languages, and, besides, I can't talk German.

These devils, I could see, all wanted to be friendly; but none of them possessed the open, frank geniality of our men. However, everyone was talking and laughing, and souvenir hunting.

I spotted a German officer, some sort of lieutenant I should think, and being a bit of a collector, I intimated to him that I had taken a fancy to some of his buttons.

We both then said things to each other which neither understood, and agreed to do a swap. I brought out my wire clippers and, with a few deft snips, removed a couple of his buttons and put them in my pocket. I then gave him two of mine in exchange.

Whilst this was going on a babbling of guttural ejaculations emanating from one of the laager-schifters, told me that some idea had occurred to someone.

Suddenly, one of the Boches ran back to his trench and presently reappeared with a large camera. I posed in a mixed group for several photographs, and have ever since wished I had fixed up some arrangement for getting a copy. No doubt framed editions of this photograph are reposing on some Hun mantelpieces, showing clearly and unmistakably to admiring strafers how a group of perfidious English surrendered unconditionally on Christmas Day to the brave Deutschers.

Slowly the meeting began to disperse; a sort of feeling that the authorities on both sides were not very enthusiastic about this fraternizing seemed to creep across the gathering. We parted, but there was a distinct and friendly understanding that Christmas Day would be left to finish in tranquillity. The last I saw of this little affair was a vision of one of my machine gunners, who was a bit of an amateur hairdresser in civil life, cutting the unnaturally long hair of a docile Boche, who was patiently kneeling on the ground whilst the automatic clippers crept up the back of his neck.

CHAPTER IX

SOUVENIRS—A RIDE TO NIEPPE—
TEA AT H.Q.—TRENCHES ONCE MORE

A couple of days after Christmas we left for billets. These two days were of a very peaceful nature, but not quite so enthusiastically friendly as the day itself. The Germans could be seen moving about in their trenches, and one felt quite at ease sitting on the top of our parapet or strolling about the fields behind our lines.

It was during these two days that I managed to get a German rifle that I had had my eye on for a month. It lay out in the open, near one or two corpses between our trenches and theirs, and until this Christmas truce arrived, the locality was not a particularly attractive one to visit. Had I fixed an earlier date for my exploit the end of it would most probably have been—a battered second-lieutenant's cap and a rusty revolver hanging up in the ingle-nook at Herr Someone-or-other's country home in East Prussia. As it was, I was able to walk out and return with the rifle unmolested.

When we left the trenches to "go out" this time I took the rifle along with me. After my usual perilous equestrian act I got back to the Transport Farm, and having performed the usual routine of washing, shaving, eating and drinking, blossomed forth into our four days' rest again.

The weather was splendid. I went out for walks in the fields, rehearsed the machine-gun section in their drill, and conducted cheery sort of

"Squire-of-the-village" conversations with the farmer who owned our farm.

At this period, most of my pals in the regiment used to go into Armentières or Bailleul, and get a breath of civilized life. I often wished I felt as they did, but I had just the opposite desire. I felt that, to adequately stick out what we were going through, it was necessary for me to keep well in the atmosphere, and not to let any exterior influence upset it.

I was annoyed at having to take up this line, but somehow or other I had a feeling that I could not run the war business with a spot of civilization in it. Personally, I felt that, rather than leave the trenches for our periodic rests, I would sooner have stayed there all the time consecutively, until I could stick it out no longer.

During this after-Christmas rest, however, I so far relapsed from these views as to decide to go into Nieppe to get some money from the Field Cashier. That was my first fall, but my second was even more strange. In a truculent tone I said I would ride!

"Smith, go and tell Parker to get my horse ready!" It just shows how reckless warfare makes one.

A beautiful, fine, still afternoon. I started off. Enormous success. I walked and trotted along, past all sorts of wagons, lorries, guns and despatch riders. Nearly decided to take up hunting, when the time came for me to settle in England once more. However, as I neared the outskirts of Nieppe, and saw the flood of interlacing traffic, I decided to leave well alone—to tie this quadruped of mine up at some outlying hostelry and walk the short remaining distance into the town where the cashier had his office. I found a suitable place and, letting myself down to the ground, strode off with a stiff bandy-legged action to the office. Having got my 100 francs all right I made the best of my short time on earth by walking about and having a good look at the town. A squalid, uninteresting place, Nieppe; a dirty red-brick town with a good sprinkling of factory chimneys and orange peel; rather the same tone as one of the Potteries towns in

England. Completing my tour I returned to the horse, and finally, stiff but happy, I glided to the ground in the yard of the Transport Farm.

Encouraged by my success I rode over to dinner one night with one of the Companies in the Battalion which was in billets about a mile and a half away. Riding home along the flat, winding, water-logged lane by the light of the stars I nearly started off on the poetry lines again, but I got home just in time.

During these rests from the trenches I was sometimes summoned to Brigade Headquarters, where the arch machine gunner dwelt. He was a captain of much engineering skill, who supervised the entire machine-gun outfit of the Brigade. New men were being perpetually trained by him, and I was sent for on occasion to discuss the state and strength of my section, or any new scheme that might be on hand.

This going to Brigade Headquarters meant putting on a clean bib, as it were; for it was here that the Brigadier himself lived, and after a machine-gun séance it was generally necessary to have tea in the farm with the Brigade staff.

I am little or no use on these social occasions. The red and gold mailed fist of a General Staff reduces me to a sort of pulverized state of meekness, which ends in my smiling at everyone and declining anything to eat.

As machine-gun officer to our Battalion I had to go through it, and as everyone was very nice to me, it all went off satisfactorily.

On this time out we were wondering how we should find the Boches on our return, and pleasant recollections of the time before filled us with a curious keenness to get back and see. A wish like this is easily gratified at the front, and soon, of course, the day came to go into trenches again, and in we went.

CHAPTER X

MY PARTIAL ESCAPE FROM THE MUD—THE DESERTED VILLAGE— MY "COTTAGE"

Our next time up after our Christmas Day experiences were full of incident and adventure. During the peace which came upon the land around the 25th of December we had, as I mentioned before, been able to stroll about in an altogether unprecedented way. We had had the courage to walk into the mangled old village just behind our front line trenches, and examine the ruins. I had never penetrated into this gloomy wreck of a place, even at night, until after Christmas. It had just occasionally caught our attention as we looked back from our trenches; mutilated and deserted, a dirty skeleton of what once had been a small village—very small—about twelve small houses and a couple of farms. Anyway, during this time in after Christmas we started thinking out plans, and in a few days we heard that it had been decided to put some men into the village, and hold it, as a second line.

The platoon commander with whom I lived happened to be the man selected to have charge of the men in the village. Consequently one night he left our humble trench and, together with his servant and small belongings from the dug-out, went off to live somewhere in the village.

About this time the conditions under which we lived were very poor. The cold and rain were exceedingly severe, and altogether physical discomfort was at its height. When my stable companion had gone I naturally determined to pay him a call the next night, and to see what sort of a place he had managed to get to live in. I well remember that next night. It was the first on which I realized the chances of a change of life presented by the village, and this was the start of two months' "village" life for me. I went off from our old trench after dusk on my usual round of the machine guns. When this was over I struck off back across the field behind our trench to the village, and waded up what had been the one and only street. Out of the dozen mangled wrecks of houses I didn't know which one my pal had chosen as his residence, so I went along the shell-mutilated, water-logged road, peering into this ruin and that, until, at the end of the street, about four hundred yards from the Germans and two hundred yards from our own trenches, I came across a damp and dark figure lurking in the shadows: "'Alt! 'oo goes there?" "Friend!" "Pass, friend, all's well." The sentry, evidently posted at end of village.

I got a tip from him as to my friend's new dwelling-place. "I say, Sentry, which house does Mr. Hudson live in?" "That small 'un down t'other end on the left, sir." "Thanks." I went back along the deserted ruin of a street, and at the far end on the left I saw the dim outline of a small cottage, almost intact it appeared, standing about five yards back from the road. This was the place the sentry meant right enough, and in I went at the hole in the plaster wall. The front door having apparently stopped something or other previously, was conspicuous by its absence.

All was dark. I groped my way along round to the back, stumbling over various bits of debris on the ground, until I found the opening into what must be the room where Hudson had elected to live. Not a light showed anywhere, which was as it should be, for a light would be easily seen by the Boches not far away, and if they did see one there would be trouble.

"Someone's been
at this blinkin Strawberry"

I came to an opening covered with an old sack. Pulling this a little to one side I was greeted with a volume of suffocating smoke. I proceeded further, and diving in under the sack, got inside the room. In the midst of the smoke, sitting beside a crushed and battered fire-bucket, sat a man, his face illuminated by the flickering light from the fire. The rest of the room was bathed in mysterious darkness. "Where's Mr. Hudson?" I asked. "He's out havin' a look at the barbed wire in front of the village, I think, sir; but he'll be back soon, as this is where 'e stays now." I determined to wait, and, to fill in the time, started to examine the cottage.

It was the first house I had been into in the firing line, and, unsavoury wreck of a place as it was, it gave one a delightful feeling of comfort to sit on the stone-flagged floor and look upon four perforated walls and a shattered roof. The worst possible house in the world would be an improvement on any of those dug-outs we had in the trenches. The front room had been blown away, leaving a back room and a couple of lean-tos which opened out from it. An attic under the thatched roof with all one end knocked out completed the outfit. The outer and inner walls were all made of that stuff known as wattle and daub—sort of earth-like plaster worked into and around hurdles. A bullet would, of course, go through walls of this sort like butter, and so they had. For, on examining the outer wall on the side which faced the Germans, I found it looking like the top of a pepper-pot for holes.

A sound as of a man trying to waltz with a cream separator, suggested to my mind that someone had tripped and fallen over that mysterious obstacle outside, which I had noticed on entering, and presently I heard Hudson's voice cursing through the sack doorway.

He came in and saw me examining the place. "Hullo, you're here too, are you?" he exclaimed. "Are you going to stay here as well?"

"I don't quite know yet," I replied. "It doesn't seem a bad idea, as I have to walk the round of all the guns the whole time; all I can and have to do is to hitch up in some central place, and this is just as central as that rotten trench we've just come from."

"Of course it is," he replied. "If I were you I'd come along and stay with me, and go to all your places from here. If an attack comes you'll be able to get from one place to another much easier than if you were stuck in that trench. You'd never be able to move from there when an attack and bombardment had started."

Having given the matter a little further consideration I decided to move from my dug-out to this cottage, so I left the village and went back across the field to the trench to see to the necessary arrangements.

I got back to my lair and shouted for my servant. "Here, Smith," I said, "I'm going to fix up at one of the houses in the village. This place of ours here is no more central than the village, and any one of those houses is a damn sight better than this clay hole here. I want you to collect all my stuff and bring it along; I'll show you the way." So presently, all my few belongings having been collected, we set out for the village. That was my last of that fearful trench. A worse one I know could not be found. My new life in the village now started, and I soon saw that it had its advantages. For instance, there was a slight chance of fencing off some of the rain and water. But my knowledge of "front" by this time was such that I knew there were corresponding disadvantages, and my instinct told me that the village would present a fresh crop of dangers and troubles quite equal to those of the trench, though slightly different in style. I had now started off on my two months' sojourn in the village of St. Yvon.

CHAPTER XI

STOCKTAKING—FORTIFYING— NEBULOUS FRAGMENTS

Hudson, myself, his servant and my servant, all crushed into that house that night. What a relief it was! We all slept in our greatcoats on the floor, which was as hard as most floors are, and dirtier than the generality; but being out of the water and able to stretch oneself at full length made up for all deficiencies. Hudson and I both slept in the perforated room; the servants in the larger chamber, near the fire bucket.

I got up just before dawn as usual, and taking advantage of the grey light, stole about the village and around the house, sizing up the locality and seeing how my position stood with regard to the various machine-gun emplacements. The dawn breaking, I had to skunk back into the house again, as it was imperative to us to keep up the effect of "Deserted house in village." We had to lurk inside all day, or if we went out, creep about with enormous caution, and go off down a slight slope at the back until we got to the edge of the wood which we knew must be invisible to the enemy. I spent this day making a thorough investigation of the house, creeping about all its component parts and thinking out how we could best utilize its little advantages. Hudson had crept out to examine the village by stealth, and I went on with plots for fortifying the "castle," and for being able to make ourselves as snug as we could in this frail shell of a cottage. I found a hole in the floor boards of the attic and pulled myself up into it thereby.

This attic, as I have said before, had all one end blown away, but the two sloping thatched sides remained. I cut a hole in one of these with my pocket-knife, and thus obtained a view of the German trenches without committing the error of looking out through the blown-out end, which would have clearly shown an observer that the house was occupied. Looking out through the slit I had made I obtained a panoramic view, more or less, of the German trenches and our own. The view, in short, was this: One saw the backs of our own trenches, then the "No man's land" space of ground, and beyond that again the front of the German trenches. This is best explained by the sketch map which I give on the opposite page. I saw exactly how the house stood with regard to the position, and also noticed that it had two dangerous sides, *i.e.*, two sides which faced the Germans, as our position formed two sides of a triangle.

I then proceeded to explore the house. In the walls I found a great many bullets which had stuck in between the bricks of the solitary chimney or imbedded themselves in the woodwork of the door or supporting posts at the corners. Amongst the straw in the attic I found a typical selection of pathetic little trifles: two pairs of very tiny clogs, evidently belonging to some child about four or five years old, one or two old and battered hats, and a quantity of spinning material and instruments. I have the small clogs at my home now, the only souvenir I have of that house at St. Yvon, which I have since learnt is no more, the Germans having reduced it to a powdered up mound of brick-dust and charred straw. Outside, and lying all around, were a miscellaneous collection of goods. Half a sewing machine, a gaudy cheap metal clock, a sort of mangle with strange wooden blades (which I subsequently cut off to make shelves with), and a host of other dirty, rain-soaked odds and ends.

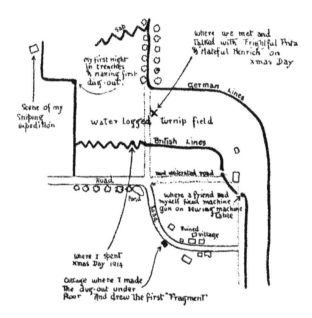

Having concluded my examination I crept out back to the wood and took a look at it all from there. "Yes," I thought to myself, "it's all very nice, but, by Gad, we'll have to look out that they don't see us, and get to think we're in this village, or they'll give us a warm time." It had gone very much against my thought-out views on trench warfare, coming to this house at all, for I had learnt by the experiences of others that the best maxim to remember was "Don't live in a house."

The reason is not far to seek. There is something very attractive to artillery about houses. They can range on them well, and they afford a more definite target than an open trench. Besides, if you can spot a house that contains, say, half a dozen to a dozen people, and just plop a "Johnson" right amidships, it generally means "exit house and people," which, I suppose, is a desirable object to be attained, according to twentieth century manners.

However, we had decided to live in the house, but as I crept back from the wood, I determined to take a few elementary and common-sense precautions. Hudson had returned when I got back, and together we discussed the house, the position, and everything we could think of in connection with the business, as we sat on the floor and had our midday meal of bully beef and biscuits, rounded up by tea and plum and apple jam spread neat from the tin on odd corners of broken biscuits. We thoroughly talked over the question of possible fortifications and precautions. I said, "What we really want is an emergency exit somewhere, where we can stand a little chance, if they start to shell us."

He agreed, and we both decided to pile up all the odd bricks, which were lying outside at the back of the house, against the perforated wall, and then sleep there in a little easier state of mind. We contented ourselves with this little precaution to begin with, but later on, as we lived in that house, we thought of larger and better ideas, and launched out into all sorts of elaborate schemes, as I will show when the time comes.

Anyway, for the first couple of sessions spent in that house in St. Yvon, we were content with merely making ourselves bullet proof. The whole day had to be spent with great caution indoors; any visit elsewhere had to be conducted with still greater caution, as the one great thing to be remembered was "Don't let 'em see we're in the village." So we had long days, just lying around in the dirty old straw and accumulated dirt of the cottage floor.

We both sat and talked and read a bit, sometimes slept, and through the opening beneath the sack across the back door we watched the evenings creeping on, and finally came the night, when we stole out like vampires and went about our trench work. It was during these long, sad days that my mind suddenly turned on making sketches. This period of my trench life marked the start of *Fragments from France*, though it was not till the end of February that a complete and presentable effort, suitable for publication in a paper, emerged. It was nothing new to me to draw, as for a very long time before the war I had drawn hundreds of sketches, and had spent a great amount of time reading and learning about all kinds of drawing and painting. I have always had an enormous interest in Art; my room at home will prove that to anyone. Stacks of bygone efforts of mine will also bear testimony to this. Yet it was not until January, 1915, that I had sufficiently resigned myself to my fate in the war, to let my mind turn to my only and most treasured hobby. In this cottage at St. Yvon the craving came back to me. I didn't fight against it, and began by making a few pencil scribbles with a joke attached, and pinned them up in our cracked shell of a room. Jokes at the expense of our miserable surroundings they were, and these were the first "Fragments." Several men in the local platoon collared these spasms, and soon after I came across them, muddy and battered, in various dug-outs near by. After these few sketches, which were done on rough bits of paper which I found lying about, I started to operate on the walls. With some bits of charcoal, I made a mess on all the four walls of our back room. There was a large circular gash, made by a spent bullet I fancy, on one of the walls, and by making it appear as though this mark was the centre point of a large explosion, I gave an apparent velocity to the figure of a German, which I drew above.

These daubs of mine provoked mirth to those who lived with me, and others who occasionally paid us visits. I persisted, and the next "masterpiece" was the figure of a soldier (afterwards Private Blobs, of "Fragments") sitting up a tree staring straight in front of him into the future, whilst a party of corpulent Boches are stalking towards him through the long grass and barbed wire. He knows there's something not quite nice going on, but doesn't like to look down. This was called "The

Listening Post," and the sensation described was so familiar to most that this again was apparently a success. So what with scribbling, reading and sleeping, not to mention time occupied in consuming plum and apple jam, bully, and other delicacies which a grateful country has ordained as the proper food for soldiers, we managed to pull through our days. Two doses of the trenches were done like this, and then came the third time up, when a sudden burst of enthusiasm and an increasing nervousness as to the safety of ourselves and our house, caused us to launch out into really trying to fortify the place. The cause of this decision to do something, to our abode was, I think, attributable to the fact that for about a fortnight the Germans had taken to treating us to a couple of dozen explosions each morning—the sort of thing one doesn't like just before breakfast; but if you've got to have it, the thing obviously to do is to try and defend yourself; so the next time, up we started.

CHAPTER XII

A BRAIN WAVE—MAKING A "FUNK HOLE" —PLUGSTREET WOOD—SNIPING

On arriving up at St. Yvon for our third time round there, we—as usual now—went into our cottage again, and the regiment spread itself out around the same old trenches. There was always a lot of work for me to do at nights, as machine guns always have to be moved as occasion arises, or if one gets a better idea for their position. By this time I had one gun in the remnant of a house about fifty yards away from our cottage. This was a reserve gun, and was there carrying out an idea of mine, *i.e.*, that it was in a central position, which would enable it to be rapidly moved to any threatened part of the line, and also it would form a bit of an asset in the event of our having to defend the village.

The section for this gun lived in the old cellar close by, and it was this cellar which gave me an idea. When I went into our cottage I searched to see if we had overlooked a cellar. No, there wasn't one. Now, then, the idea. I thought, "Why not make a cellar, and thus have a place to dive into when the strafing begins." After this terrific outburst of sagacity I sat down in a corner and, with a biscuitload of jam, discussed my scheme with my platoon-commander pal. We agreed it was a good idea. I was feeling energetic, and always liking a little tinkering on my own, I said I would make it myself.

So Hudson retired into the lean-to and I commenced to plot this engineering project. I scraped away as much as necessary of the accumulated filth on the floor, and my knife striking something hard I found it to be tiles. Up till then I had always imagined it to be an earth floor, but tiled it was right enough—large, square, dark red ones of a very rough kind. I called for Smith, my servant, and telling him to bring his entrenching tool, I began to prize up some of the tiles. It wasn't very easy, fitting the blade of the entrenching tool into the crevices, but once I had got a start and had got one or two out, things were easier.

I pulled up all the tiles along one wall about eight feet long and out into the room a distance of about four feet. I now had a bare patch of hard earth eight feet by four to contend with. Luckily we had a pickaxe and a shovel lying out behind the house, so taking off my sheepskin jacket and balaclava, I started off to excavate the hole which I proposed should form a sort of cellar.

It was a big job, and my servant and I were hard at it, turn and turn about, the whole of that day. A dull, rainy day, a cold wind blowing the old sack about in the doorway, and in the semi-darkness inside yours truly handing up Belgian soil on a war-worn shovel to my servant, who held a sandbag perpetually open to receive it. A long and arduous job it was, and one in which I was precious near thinking that danger is preferable to digging. Mr. Doan, with his back-ache pills, would have done well if he had sent one of his travellers with samples round there that night. However, at the end of two days, I had got a really good hole delved out, and now I was getting near the more interesting feature, namely, putting a roof on, and finally being able to live in this under-ground dug-out.

This roof was perhaps rather unique as roofs go. It was a large mattress with wooden sides, a kind of oblong box with a mattress top. I found it outside in a ruined cottage. Underneath the mattress part was a cavity filled with spiral springs. I arranged a pile of sandbags at each side of the hole in the floor in such a way as to be able to lay this curiosity on top to form a roof, the mattress part downwards. I then filled in with earth all the parts where the spiral springs were placed. Total result—a roof a foot thick of earth, with a good backbone of iron springs. I often afterwards wished that that mattress had been filleted, as the spiral springs had a nasty way of bursting through the striped cover and coming at you like the lid of a Jack-in-the-box. However, such is war.

Above this roof I determined to pile up sandbags against the wall, right away up to the roof of the cottage.

This necessitated about forty sandbags being filled, so it may easily be imagined we didn't do this all at once.

However, in time, it was done—I mean after we had paid one or two more visits to the trenches.

We all felt safer after these efforts. I think we were a bit safer, but not much. I mean that we were fairly all right against anything but a direct hit, and as we knew from which direction direct hits had to come, we made that wall as thick as possible. We could, I think, have smiled at a direct hit from an 18-pounder, provided we had been down our funk hole at the time; but, of course, a direct hit from a "Johnson" would have snuffed us completely (mattress and all).

Life in this house and in the village was much more interesting and energetic than in that old trench. It was possible, by observing great caution, to creep out of the house by day and dodge about our position a bit, crawl up to points of vantage and survey the scene. Behind the cottage lay the wood—the great Bois de Ploegstert—and this in itself repaid a visit. In the early months of 1915 this wood was in a pretty mauled-about state, and as time went on of course got more so. It was full of old trenches, filled with water, relies of the period when we turned the Germans out of it. Shattered trees and old barbed wire in a solution of mud was the chief effect produced by the parts nearest the trenches, but further back "Plugstreet Wood" was quite a pretty place to walk about in. Birds singing all around, and rabbits darting about the tangled undergrowth. Long paths had been cut through the wood leading to the various parts of the trenches in front. A very quaint place, take it all in all, and one which has left a curious and not unpleasing impression on my mind.

This ability to wander around and creep about various parts of our position, led to my getting an idea, which nearly finished my life in the cottage, village, or even Belgium. I suddenly got bitten with the sniping fever, and it occurred to me that, with my facilities for getting about, I could get into a certain mangled farm on our left and remain in the roof unseen in daylight. From there I felt sure that, with the aid of a rifle, I could tickle up a Boche or two in their trenches hard by. I was immensely taken with this idea. So, one morning (like Robinson Crusoe again) I set off with my fowling-piece and ammunition, and crawled towards the farm. I got there all right, and entering the dark and evil-smelling precincts, searched around for a suitable sniping post. I saw a beam overhead in a corner from which, if I could get on to it, I felt sure I should obtain a view of the enemy trenches through a gap in the tiled roof. I tied a bit of string to my rifle and then jumping for the beam, scrambled up on it and pulled the rifle up after me. When my heart pulsations had come down to a reasonable figure I peered out through the hole in the tiles. An excellent view! The German parapet a hundred yards away! Splendid!

Now I felt sure I should see a Boche moving about or something; or I might possibly spot one looking over the top.

I waited a long time on that beam, with my loaded rifle lying in front of me. I was just getting fed up with the waiting, and about to go away, when I thought I saw a movement in the trench opposite. Yes! it was. I saw the handle of something like a broom or a water scoop moving above the sandbags. Heart doing overtime again! Most exciting! I felt convinced I should see a Boche before long. And then, at last, I saw one—or rather I caught a glimpse of a hat appearing above the line of the parapet. One of those small circular cloth hats of theirs with the two trouser buttons in front.

Up it came, and I saw it stand out nice and clear against the skyline. I carefully raised my rifle, took a steady aim, and fired. I looked: disappearance of hat! I ejected the empty cartridge case, and was just about to reload when, whizz, whistle, bang, crash! a shell came right at the farm, and exploded in the courtyard behind. I stopped short on the beam. Whizz, whistle, bang, crash! Another, right into the old cowshed on my left. Without waiting for any more I just slithered down off that beam, grabbed my rifle and dashing out across the yard back into the ditch beyond, started hastily scrambling along towards the end of one of our trenches. As I went I heard four more shells crash into that farm. It was at this moment that I coined the title of one of my sketches, "They've evidently seen me," for which I afterwards drew the picture near Wulverghem. I got back to our cottage, crawled into the hole in the floor, and thought things over. They must have seen the flash of my rifle through the tiles, and, suspecting possible sniping from the farm, must have wired back to their artillery, "Snipingberg from farmenhausen hoch!" or words to that effect.

Altogether a very objectionable episode.

CHAPTER XIII

ROBINSON CRUSOE— THAT TURBULENT TABLE

By this time we had really got our little house quite snug. A hole in the floor, a three-legged chair, and brown paper pushed into the largest of the holes in the walls—what more could a man want? However, we did want something more, and that was a table. One gets tired of balancing tins of pl—(nearly said it again)—marmalade on one's knee and holding an enamel cup in one hand and a pocket-knife in the other. So we all said how nice a table would be. I determined to say no more, but to show by deeds, not by words, that I would find a table and have one there by the next day, like a fairy in a pantomime. I started off on my search one night. Take it from me—a fairy's is a poor job out there, and when you've read the next bit you'll agree.

Behind our position stood the old ruined chateau, and beyond it one or two scattered cottages. I had never really had a good look at all at that part, and as I knew some of our reserve trenches ran around there, and that it would be a good thing to know all about them, I decided to ask the Colonel for permission to creep off one afternoon and explore the whole thing; incidentally I might by good luck find a table. It was possible, by wriggling up a mud valley and crawling over a few scattered remnants of houses and bygone trenches to reach the Colonel's headquarter dug-out in daytime. So I did it, and asked leave to go off back to have a look at the chateau and the land about it. He gave me permission, so armed with my long walking-stick (a billiard cue with the thin part cut off, which I found on passing another chateau one night) I started off to explore.

I reached the chateau. An interesting sight it was. How many shells had hit it one couldn't even guess, but the results indicated a good few. What once had been well-kept lawns were now covered with articles which would have been much better left in their proper places. One suddenly came upon half a statue of Minerva or Venus wrapped in three-quarters of a stair carpet in the middle of one of the greenhouses. Passing on, one would find the lightning conductor projecting out through the tapestried seat of a Louis Quinze chair. I never saw such a mess.

Inside, the upstairs rooms were competing with the ground-floor ones, as to which should get into the cellars first. It was really too terrible to contemplate the fearful destruction.

I found it impossible to examine much of the interior of the chateau, as blocks of masonry and twisted iron girders closed up most of the doors and passages. I left this melancholy ruin, full of thought, and proceeded across the shell-pitted gardens towards the few little cottages beyond. These were in a better state of preservation, and were well worth a visit. In the first one I entered I found a table! the very thing I wanted. It was stuck away in a small lean-to at the back. A nice little green one, just the size to suit us.

I determined to get it back to our shack somehow, but before doing so went on rummaging about these cottages. In the second cottage I made an enormously lucky find for us. Under a heap of firewood in an outhouse I found a large pile of coal. This was splendid, and would be invaluable to us and our fire-bucket. Nothing pleased me more than this, as the cold was very severe, and a fire meant so much to us. When I had completed my investigations and turned over all the oddments lying about to see if there was anything else of use to us, I started off on the return journey. It was now dark, and I was able to walk along without fear of being seen. Of course, I was taking the table with me. I decided to come back later for the coal, with a few sandbags for filling, so I covered it over and hid it as much as possible. (Sensation: Ali Baba returns from the forest.) I started off with the table. I had about three-quarters of a mile to go. Every hundred yards I had to sit down and rest. A table is a horrible thing to accompany one on a mile walk.

I reached the chateau again, and out into the fields beyond, resting with my burden about three times before I got to the road which led straight on to our trenches. My task was a bit harder now, as I was in full view of the German trenches. Had it been daylight they could have seen me quite easily.

Fortunately it was dark, but, of course, star shells would show one up quite distinctly. I staggered on down the road with the green table on my back, pausing as little as possible, but a rest had to be taken, and this at a very exposed part of the road. I put the table down and sat panting on the top. A white streak shot into the air—a star shell. Curse! I sprang off the green top and waltzed with my four-legged wooden octopus into the ditch at the side, where I lay still, waiting for the light to die out. Suspense over. I went on again.

At last I got back with that table and pushed it into our hovel under the sack doorway.

Immense success! "Just the thing we wanted!"

We all sat down to dinner that night in the approved fashion, whilst I, with the air of a conspirator, narrated the incredible story of the vast Eldorado of coal which I had discovered, and, over our shrimp paste and biscuits we discussed plans for its removal.

That frozen turnip-field-for-a-home
sensation

"Take away me ~~rank~~ and honour,
but give me a bag of coke."

CHAPTER XIV

THE AMPHIBIANS—FED UP, BUT DETERMINED—THE GUN PARAPET

So you see, life in our cottage was quite interesting and adventurous in its way. At night our existence was just the same as before; all the normal work of trench life. Making improvements to our trenches led to endless work with sandbags, planks, dug-outs, etc. My particular job was mostly improving machine-gun positions, or selecting new sites and carrying out removals,

"BRUCE BAIRNSFATHER.
MACHINE GUNS REMOVED AT SHORTEST NOTICE.
ATTACKS QUOTED FOR."

And so the long dark dreary nights went on. The men garrisoning the little cracked-up village lived mostly in cellars. Often on my rounds, during a rainy, windy, mournful night, I would look into a cellar and see a congested mass of men playing cards by the light of a candle stuck on a tin lid. A favourite form of illumination I came across was a lamp made out of an empty tobacco tin, rifle oil for the illuminant, and a bit of a shirt for a wick!

People who read all these yarns of mine, and who have known the war in later days, will say, "Ah, how very different it was then to now." In my last experiences in the war I have watched the enormous changes creeping in. They began about July, 1915. My experiences since that date were very interesting; but I found that much of the romance had left the trenches. The old days, from the beginning to July, 1915, were all so delightfully precarious and primitive. Amateurish trenches and rough and ready life, which to my mind gave this war what it sadly needs—a touch of romance.

Way back there, in about January, 1915, our soldiers had a perfectly unique test of human endurance against appalling climatic conditions. They lived in a vast bog, without being able to utilize modern contrivances for making the tight against adverse conditions anything like an equal contest. And yet I wouldn't have missed that time for anything, and I'm sure they wouldn't either.

Those who have not actually had to experience it, or have not had the opportunity to see what our men "stuck out" in those days, will never fully grasp the reality.

One night a company commander came to me in the village and told me he had got a bit of trench under his control which was altogether impossible to hold, and he wanted me to come along with him to look at it, and see if I could do anything in the way of holding the position by machine guns. His idea was that possibly a gun might be fixed in such a place behind so as to cover the frontage occupied by this trench. I came along with him to have a look and see what could be done. He and I went up the rain-soaked village street and out on to the field beyond. It was as dark as pitch, and about 11 p.m. Occasional shots cracked out of the darkness ahead from the German trenches, and I remember one in particular that woke us up a bit. A kind of derelict road-roller stood at one side of the field, and as we passed this, walking pretty close together, a bullet whizzed between us. I don't know which head it was nearest to, but it was quite near enough for both of us. We went on across the field for about two hundred yards, out towards a pile of ruins which had once been a barn, and which stood between our lines and the Germans.

Near this lay the trench which he had been telling me about. It was quite the worst I have ever seen. A number of men were in it, standing and leaning, silently enduring the following conditions. It was quite dark. The enemy was about two hundred yards away, or rather less. It was raining, and the trench contained over three feet of water. The men, therefore, were standing up to the waist in water. The front parapet was nothing but a rough earth mound which, owing to the water about, was practically non-existent. Their rifles lay on the saturated mound in front. They were all wet through and through, with a great deal of their equipment below the water at the bottom of the trench. There they were, taking it all as a necessary part of the great game; not a grumble nor a comment.

The company commander and I at once set about scheming out an alternative plan. Some little distance back we found a cellar which had once been below a house. Now there was no house, so by standing in the cellar one got a view along the ground and level with it. This was the very place for a machine gun. So we decided on fixing one there and making a sort of roof over a portion of the cellar for the gunners to live in. After about a couple of hours' work we completed this arrangement, and then removed the men, who, it was arranged, should leave the trenches that night and go back to our billets for a rest, till the next time up. We weren't quite content with the total safety of our one gun in that cellar, so we started off on a further idea.

Our trenches bulged out in a bit of a salient to the right of the rotten trench, and we decided to mount another gun at a certain projection in our lines so as to enfilade the land across which the other gun would fire.

On inspecting the projected site we found it was necessary to make rather an abnormally high parapet to stand the gun on. No sandbags to spare, of course, so the question was, "What shall we make a parapet of?"

We plodded off back to the village and groped around the ruins for something solid and high enough to carry the gun. After about an hour's climbing about amongst debris in the dark, and hauling ourselves up into remnants of attics, etc., we came upon a sewing machine. It was one of that sort that's stuck on a wooden table with a treadle arrangement underneath. We saw an idea at a glance. Pull off the sewing machine, and use the table. It was nearly high enough, and with just three or four sandbags we felt certain it would do. We performed the necessary surgical operation on the machine, and taking it in turns, padded off down to the front line trench. We had a bit of a job with that table. The parapet was a jumbled assortment of sandbags, clay, and old bricks from the neighbouring barn: but we finally got a good sound parapet made, and in about another hour's time had fixed a machine gun, with plenty of ammunition, in a very unattractive position from the Boche point of view. We all now felt better, and I'm certain that the men who held that trench felt better too. But I am equally certain that they would have stayed there *ad lib* even if we hadn't thought of and carried out an alternative arrangement. A few more nights of rain, danger and discomfort, then the time would come for us to be relieved, and those same men would be back at billets, laughing, talking and smoking, buoyant as ever.

CHAPTER XV

ARRIVAL OF THE "JOHNSONS"— "WHERE DID THAT ONE GO?"— THE FIRST FRAGMENT DISPATCHED— THE EXODUS—WHERE?

Shortly after these events we experienced rather a nasty time in the village. It had been decided, way back somewhere at headquarters, that it was essential to hold the village in a stronger way than we had been doing. More men were to be kept there, and a series of trenches dug in and around it, thus forming means for an adequate defence should disaster befall our front line trenches, which lay out on a radius of about five hundred yards from the centre of the village. This meant working parties at night, and a pretty considerable collection of soldiers lurking in cavities in various ruined buildings by day.

Anyone will know that when a lot of soldiers congregate in a place it is almost impossible to prevent someone or other being seen, or smoke from some fire showing, or, even worse, a light visible at night from some imperfectly shuttered house.

At all events, something or other gave the Boches the tip, and we soon knew they had got their attention on our village.

Each morning as we clustered round our little green table and had our breakfast, we invariably had about half a dozen rounds of 18-pounders crash around us with varying results, but one day, as we'd finished our meal and all sat staring into the future, we suddenly caught the sound of something on more corpulent lines arriving. That ponderous, slow rotating whistle of a "Johnson" caught our well-trained ears; a pause! then a reverberating, hollow-sounding "crumph!" We looked at each other.

"Heavies!" we all exclaimed.

"Look out! here comes another!" and sure enough there it was, that gargling crescendo of a whistle followed by a mighty crash, considerably nearer.

We soon decided that our best plan was to get out of the house, and stay in the ditch twenty yards away until it was over.

A house is an unwholesome spot to be in when there's shelling about. Our funk hole was all right for whizz-bangs and other fireworks of that sort, but no use against these portmanteaux they were now sending along.

Well, to resume; they put thirteen heavies into that village in pretty quick time. One old ruin was set on fire, and I felt the consequent results would be worse than just losing the building; as all the men in it had to rush outside and keep darting in and out through the flames and smoke, trying to save their rifles and equipment.

After a bit we returned into the house—a trifle prematurely, I'm afraid—as presently a pretty large line in explosive drainpipes landed close outside, and, as we afterwards discovered, blew out a fair-sized duck pond in the road. We were all inside, and I think nearly every one said a sentence which gave me my first idea for a *Fragment from France*. A sentence which must have been said countless times in this war, *i.e.*, "Where did that one go?"

We were all inside the cottage now, with intent, staring faces, looking outside through the battered doorway. There was something in the whole situation which struck me as so pathetically amusing, that when the ardour of the Boches had calmed down a bit, I proceeded to make a pencil sketch of the situation. When I got back to billets the next time I determined to make a finished wash drawing of the scene, and send it to some paper or other in England. In due course we got back to billets, and the next morning I fished out my scanty drawing materials from my valise, and sitting at a circular table in one of the rooms at the farm, I did a finished drawing of "Where did that one go," occasionally looking through the window on to a mountain of manure outside for inspiration.

The next thing was to send it off. What paper should I send it to? I had had a collection of papers sent out to me at Christmas time from some one or other. A few of these were still lying about. A *Bystander* was amongst them. I turned over the pages and considered for a bit whether my illustrated joke might be in their line. I thought of several other papers, but on the whole concluded that the *Bystander* would suit for the purpose, and so, having got the address off the cover, I packed up my drawing round a roll of old paper, enclosed it in brown paper, and put it out to be posted at the next opportunity. In due course it went to the post, and I went to the trenches again, forgetting all about the incident.

Next time in the trenches was full of excitement. We had done a couple of days of the endless mud, rain, and bullet-dodging work when suddenly one night we heard we were to be relieved and go elsewhere. Every one then thought of only one thing—where were we going? We all had different ideas. Some said we were bound for Ypres, which we heard at that time was a pretty "warm" spot; some said La Bassee was our destination—"warm," but not quite as much so as Ypres. Wild rumours that we were going to Egypt were of course around; they always are. There was another beauty: that we were going back to England for a rest!

The night after the news, another battalion arrived, and, after handing over our trenches, we started off on the road to "Somewhere in France." It was about 11.30 p.m. before we had handed over everything and finally parted from those old trenches of ours. I said good-bye to our little perforated hovel, and set off with all my machine gunners and guns for the road behind the wood, to go—goodness knows where. We looked back over our shoulders several times as we plodded along down the muddy road and into the corduroy path which ran through the wood. There, behind us, lay St. Yvon, under the moonlight and drifting clouds; a silhouetted mass of ruins beyond the edge of the wood. Still the same old intermittent cracking of the rifle shots and the occasional star shell. It was quite sad parting with that old evil-smelling, rain-soaked scene of desolation. We felt how comfortable we had all been there, now that we were leaving. And leaving for what?—that was the question. When I reached the road, and had superintended loading up our limbers, I got instructions from the transport officer as to which way we were to go. The battalion had already gone on ahead, and the machine-gun section was the last to leave. We were to go down the road to Armentières, and at about twelve midnight we started on our march, rattling off down the road leading to Armentières, bound for some place we had never seen before. At about 2 a.m. we got there; billets had been arranged for us, but at two in the morning it was no easy task to find the quarters allotted to us without the assistance of a guide. The battalion had got there first, had found their billets and gone to bed. I and the machine-gun section rattled over the cobbles into sleeping Armentières, and hadn't the slightest idea where we had to go. Nobody being about to tell us, we paraded the town like a circus procession for about an hour before finally finding out where we were to billet, and ultimately we reached our destination when, turning into the barns allotted to us, we made the most of what remained of the night in well-earned repose.

CHAPTER XVI

NEW TRENCHES—THE NIGHT INSPECTION—LETTER FROM THE "BYSTANDER"

Next day we discovered the mystery of our sudden removal. The battle of Neuve Chapelle was claiming considerable attention, and that was where we were going. We were full of interest and curiosity, and were all for getting there as soon as possible. But it was not to be. Mysterious moves were being made behind the scenes which I, and others like me, will never know anything about; but, anyway, we now suddenly got another bewildering order. After a day spent in Armentières we were told to stand by for going back towards Neuve Eglise again, just the direction from which we had come. We all knew too much about the war to be surprised at anything, so we mutely prepared for another exit. It was a daylight march this time, and a nice, still, warm day. Quite a cheery, interesting march we had, too, along the road from Armentières to Neuve Eglise. We were told that we were to march past General Sir Horace Smith Dorrien, whom we should find waiting for us near the Pont de Nieppe—a place we had to pass *en route*. Every one braced up at this, and keenly looked forward to reaching Nieppe. I don't know why, but I had an idea he would be in his car on the right of the road. To make no mistake I muttered "Eyes right" to myself for about a quarter of a mile, so as to make a good thing of the salute. We came upon the Pont de Nieppe suddenly, round the corner, and there was the General—on the left! All my rehearsing useless. Annoying, but I suppose one can't expect Generals to tell you where they are going to stand.

We reached Neuve Eglise in time, and went into our old billets. We all thought our fate was "back into those—old Plugstreet trenches again," but *mirabile dictu*—it was not to be so. The second day in billets I received a message from the Colonel to proceed to his headquarter farm. I went, and heard the news. We were to take over a new line of trenches away to the left of Plugstreet, and that night I was to accompany him along with all the company commanders on a round of inspection.

A little before dusk we started off and proceeded along various roads towards the new line. All the country was now brand new to me, and full of interest. After we had gone about a mile and a half the character of the land changed. We had left all the Plugstreet wood effect behind, and now emerged on to far more open and flatter ground. By dusk we were going down a long straight road with poplar trees on either side. At the end of this stood a farm on the right. We walked into the courtyard and across it into the farm. This was the place the battalion we were going to relieve had made its headquarters. Not a bad farm. The roof was still on, I noticed, and concluded from that that life there was evidently passable. We had to wait here some time, as we were told that the enemy could see for a great distance around there, and would pepper up the farm as sure as fate if they saw anyone about. Our easy-going entry into the courtyard had not been received with great favour, as it appeared we were doing just the very thing to get the roof removed. However, the dusk had saved us, I fancy.

As soon as it was really dark we all sallied forth, accompanied by guides this time, who were to show us the trenches. I crept along behind our Colonel, with my eyes peeled for possible gun positions, and drinking in as many details of the entire situation as I could.

We walked about ten miles that night, I should think, across unfamiliar swamps and over unsuspected antique abandoned trenches, past dead cows and pigs. We groped about the wretched shell-pitted fields, examining the trenches we were about to take over. You would be surprised to find how difficult a simple line of trenches can seem at night if you have never seen them before.

"Comin' an down to the Estaminet tonight Arry?"

You don't seem able to get the angles, somehow, nor to grasp how the whole situation faces, or how you get from one part to another, and all that sort of thing. I know that by the time I had been along the whole lot, round several hundred traverses, and up dozens of communication trenches and saps, all my mariner-like ability for finding my way back to Neuve Eglise had deserted me. Those guides were absolutely necessary in order to get us back to the headquarter farm. One wants a compass, the pole star, and plenty of hope ever to get across those enormous prairies—known as fields out there—and reach the place at the other side one wants to get to. It is a long study before you really learn the simplest and best way up to your own bit of trench; but when it comes to learning everybody else's way up as well (as a machine gunner has to), it needs a long and painful course of instruction—higher branches of this art consisting of not only knowing the way up, but the *safest* way up.

The night we carried out this tour of inspection we were all left in a fog as to how we had gone to and returned from the trenches. After we had got in we knew, by long examination of the maps, how everything lay, but it was some time before we had got the real practical hang of it all.

Our return journey from the inspection was a pretty silent affair. We all knew these were a nasty set of trenches. Not half so pleasant as the Plugstreet ones. The conversations we had with the present owners made it quite clear that warm times were the vogue round there. Altogether we could see we were in for a "bit of a time."

We cleared off back to Neuve Eglise that night, and next day took those trenches over. This was the beginning of my life at Wulverghem. When we got in, late that night, we found that the post had arrived some time before. Thinking there might be something for me, I went into the back room where they sorted the letters, to get any there might be before going off to my own billets. "There's only one for you, sir, to-night," said the corporal who looked after the letters. He handed me an envelope. I opened it. Inside, a short note and a cheque.

"We shall be very glad to accept your sketch, 'Where did that one go to?' From the *Bystander*"—the foundation-stone of *Fragments from France*.

CHAPTER XVII

WULVERGHEM—THE DOUVE— CORDUROY BOARDS—BACK AT OUR FARM

We got out of the frying-pan into the fire when we went to Wulverghem—a much more exciting and precarious locality than Plugstreet. During all my war experiences I have grown to regard Plugstreet as the unit of tranquillity. I have never had the fortune to return there since those times mentioned in previous chapters. When you leave Plugstreet you take away a pleasing memory of slime and reasonable shelling, which is more than you can say for the other places. If you went to Plugstreet after, say, the Ypres Salient, it would be more or less like going to a convalescent home after a painful operation.

But, however that may be, we were now booked for Wulverghem, or rather the trenches which lie along the base of the Messines ridge, about a mile in front of that shattered hamlet. Two days after our tour of inspection we started off to take over. The nuisance about these trenches was that the point where one had to unload and proceed across country, man-handling everything, was abnormally far away from the firing line. We had about a mile and a half to do after we had marched collectively as a battalion, so that my machine-gunners were obliged to carry the guns and all the tackle we needed all that distance to their trenches. This, of course, happened every time we "came in."

The land where these trenches lay was a vast and lugubrious expanse of mud, with here and there a charred and ragged building. On our right lay the River Douve, and, on our left, the trenches turned a corner back inwards again. In front lay the long line of the Messines ridge. The Boches had occupied this ridge, and our trenches ran along the valley at its foot. The view which the Boches got by being perched on this hill rendered them exactly what their soul delights in, *i.e.*, "uber alles." They can see for miles. However, those little disadvantages have not prevented us from efficiently maintaining our trenches at the far end of the plain, in spite of the difficulty of carrying material across this flat expanse.

I forget what night of the week we went in and took over those trenches, but, anyhow, it was a precious long one. I had only seen the place once before, and in the darkness of the night had a long and arduous job finding the way to the various positions allotted for my guns, burdened as I was with all my sections and impedimenta. I imagine I walked about five or six miles that night. We held a front of about a mile, and, therefore, not only did I have to do the above-mentioned mile and a half, but also two or three miles going from end to end of our line. It was as dark as could be, and the unfamiliar ground seemed to be pitted like a Gruyère cheese with shell holes. Unlimbering back near a farm we sloshed off across the mud flat towards the section of trench which we had been ordered to occupy. I trusted to instinct to strike the right angles for coming out at the trenches which henceforth were to be ours. In those days my machine guns were the old type of Maxim—a very weighty concern. To carry these guns and all the necessary ammunition across this desert was a long and very exhausting process. Occasional bursts of machine-gun fire and spent bullets "zipping" into the mud all around hardly tended to cheer the proceedings. The path along to the right-hand set of trenches, where I knew a couple of guns must go, was lavishly strewn with dead cows and pigs. When we paused for a rest we always seemed to do so alongside some such object, and consequently there was no hesitation in moving on again. None of us had the slightest idea as to the nature of the country on which we were now operating. I myself had only seen it by night, and nobody else had been there at all.

The commencement of the journey from the farm of disembarkation lay along what is known as corduroy boards. These are short, rough, wooden planks, nailed crossways on long baulks of timber. This kind of path is a very popular one at the front, and has proved an immense aid in saving the British army from being swallowed up in the mud.

The corduroy path ran out about four hundred yards across the grassless, sodden field. We then came suddenly to the beginning of a road. A small cottage stood on the right, and in front of it a dead cow. Here we unfortunately paused, but almost immediately moved on (gas masks weren't introduced until much later!).

From this point the road ran in a long straight line towards Messines. At intervals, on the right-hand side only, stood one or two farms, or, rather, their skeletons. As we went along in the darkness these farms silhouetted their dreary remains against the faint light in the sky, and looked like vast decayed wrecks of antique Spanish galleons upside down. On past these farms the road was suddenly cut across by a deep and ugly gash: a reserve trench. So now we were getting nearer to our destination. A particularly large and evil-smelling farm stood on the right. The reserve trench ran into its back yard, and disappeared amongst the ruins. From the observations I had made, when inspecting these trenches, I knew that the extreme right of our position was a bit to the right of this farm, so I and my performing troupe decided to go through the farmyard and out diagonally across the field in front. We did this, and at last could dimly discern the line of the trenches in front. We were now on the extreme right of the section we had to control, close to the River Douve, and away to the left ran the whole line of our trenches. Along the whole length of this line the business of taking over from the old battalion was being enacted. That old battalion made a good bargain when they handed over that lot of slots to us. The trenches lay in a sort of echelon formation, the one on the extreme right being the most advanced. This one we made for, and as we squelched across the mud to it a couple of German star shells fizzed up into the air and illuminated the whole scene. By their light I could see the whole position, but could only form an approximate idea of how our lines ran, as our parapets and trenches merged into the mud so effectively as to look like a vast, tangled, disorderly mass of sandbags, slime and shell holes. We reached the right-hand trench. It was a curious sort of a trench too, quite a different pattern to those we had occupied at St. Yvon, The first thing that struck me about all these trenches was the quantity of sandbags there were, and the geometrical exactness of the attempts at traverses, fire steps, bays, etc. Altogether, theoretically, much superior trenches, although very cramped and narrow. I waited for another star shell in order to see the view out in front. One hadn't long to wait around there for star shells. One very soon sailed up, nice and white, into the inky sky, and I saw how we were placed with regard to the Germans, the hill and Messines. We were quite near a little stream, a tributary of the Douve, in fact it ran along the front of our trenches. Immediately on the other side the ground rose in a gradual slope up the Messines hill, and about three-quarters way up this slope were the German trenches.

When I had settled the affairs of the machine guns in the right-hand trench I went along the line and fixed up the various machine-gun teams in the different trenches as I came to them. The ground above the trenches was so eaten away by the filling of sandbags and the cavities caused by shell fire, that I found it far quicker and simpler to walk along in the trenches themselves, squeezing past the men standing about and around the thick traverses. Our total frontal length must have been three-quarters of a mile, I should think. This, our first night in, was a pretty busy one. Dug-outs had to be found to accommodate every one; platoons arranged in all the sections of trench, all the hundred-and-one details which go to making trench life as secure and comfortable as is possible under the circumstances, had to be seen to and arranged. I had fixed up all the sections by about ten o'clock and then started along the lines again trying to get as clear an idea as possible of the entire situation of the trenches, the type of land in front of each, the means of access to each trench, and possible improvements in the various gun positions. All this had to be done to the accompaniment of a pretty lively mixture of bullets and star shells. Sniping was pretty severe that night, and, indeed, all the time we were in those Douve trenches. There was an almost perpetual succession of rifle shots, intermingled with the rapid crackling of machine-gun fire. However, you soon learn out there that you can just as easily "get one" on the calmest night by an accidental spent bullet as you can when a little hate is on, and bullets are coming thick and fast. The first night we came to the Douve was a pretty calm one, comparatively speaking; yet one poor chap in the leading platoon, going through the farm courtyard I mentioned, got shot right through the forehead. No doubt whatever it was an accidental bullet, and not an aimed shot, as the Germans could not have possibly seen the farm owing to the darkness of the night.

Just as I was finishing my tour of inspection I came across the Colonel, who was going round everything, and thoroughly reconnoitring the position. He asked me to show him the gun positions. I went with him right along the line. We stood about on parapets, and walked all over the place, stopping motionless now and again as a star shell went up, and moving on again just in time to hear a bullet or two whizz past behind and go "smack" into a tree in the hedge behind, or "plop" into the mud parados. When the Colonel had finished his tour of inspection he asked me to walk back with him to his headquarters. "Where are you living, Bairnsfather?" said the Colonel to me. "I don't know, sir," I replied. "I thought of fixing up in that farm (I indicated the most aromatized one by the reserve trench) and making some sort of a dug-out if there isn't a cellar; it's a fairly central position for all the trenches."

The Colonel thought for a moment: "You'd better come along back to the farm on the road for to-night anyway, and you can spend to-morrow decorating the walls with a few sketches," he said. This was a decidedly better suggestion, a reprieve, in fact, as prior to this remark my bedroom for the night looked like being a borrowed ground sheet slung over some charred rafters which were leaning against a wall in the yard.

I followed along behind the Colonel down the road, down the corduroy boards, and out at the old moated farm not far from Wulverghem. Thank goodness, I should get a floor to sleep on! A roof, too! Straw on the floor! How splendid!

It was quite delightful turning into that farm courtyard, and entering the building. Dark, dismal and deserted as it was, it afforded an immense, glowing feeling of comfort after that mysterious, dark and wintry plain, with its long lines of grey trenches soaking away there under the inky sky.

Inside I found an empty room with some straw on the floor. There was only one shell hole in it, but some previous tenant had stopped it up with a bit of sacking. My word, I was tired! I rolled myself round with straw, and still retaining all my clothes, greatcoat, balaclava, muffler, trench boots, I went to sleep.

CHAPTER XVIII

THE PAINTER AND DECORATOR— FRAGMENTS FORMING—NIGHT ON THE MUD PRAIRIE

Had a fairly peaceful night. I say fairly because when one has to get up three or four times to see whether the accumulated rattle of rifle fire is going to lead to a battle, or turn out only to be merely "wind up," it rather disturbs one's rest. You see, had an attack of some sort come on, yours truly would have had to run about a mile and a half to some central spot to overlook the machine-gun department. I used to think that to be actually with one gun was the best idea, but I subsequently found that this plan hampered me considerably from getting to my others; the reason being that, once established in one spot during an open trench attack, it is practically impossible to get to another part whilst the action is on.

At the Douve, however, I discovered a way of getting round this which I will describe later.

On this first night, not being very familiar with the neighbourhood, I found it difficult to ignore the weird noises which floated in through the sack-covered hole. There is something very eerie and strange about echoing rifle shots in the silence of the night. Once I got up and walked out into the courtyard of the farm, and passing through it came out on to the end of the road. All as still as still could be, except the distant intermittent cracking of the rifles coming from away across the plain, beyond the long straight row of lofty poplar trees which marked the road. A silence of some length might supervene, in which one would only hear the gentle rustling of the leaves; then suddenly, far away on the right, a faint surging roar can be heard, and then louder and louder. "Wind up over there." Then, gradually, silence would assert itself once more and leave you with nothing but the rustling leaves and the crack of the sniper's rifle on the Messines ridge.

My first morning at this farm was, by special request, to be spent in decorating the walls.

There wasn't much for anyone to do in the day time, as nobody could go out. The same complaint as the other place in St. Yvon: "We mustn't look as if anyone lives in the farm." Drawing, therefore, was a great aid to me in passing the day. Whilst at breakfast I made a casual examination of the room where we had our meals. I was not the first to draw on the walls of that room. Some one in a previous battalion had already put three or four sketches on various parts of the fire-place. Several large spaces remained all round the room, however; but I noticed that the surface was very poor compared with the wall round the fire-place.

The main surface was a rough sort of thing, and, on regarding it closely, it looked as if it was made of frozen porridge, being slightly rough, and of a grey-brown colour. I didn't know what on earth I could use to draw on this surface, but after breakfast I started to scheme out something. I went into the back room, which we were now using as a kitchen, and finding some charcoal I tried that. It was quite useless—wouldn't make a mark on the wall at all. Why, I don't know; but the charcoal just glided about and merely seemed to make dents and scratches on the "frozen porridge." I then tried to make up a mixture. It occurred to me that possibly soot might be made into a sort of ink, and used with a paint brush. I tried this, but drew a blank again. I was bordering on despair, when my servant said he thought he had put a bottle of Indian ink in my pack when we left to come into the trenches this time. He had a look, and found that his conjecture was right; he had got a bottle of Indian ink

112

and a few brushes, as he thought I might want to draw something, so had equipped the pack accordingly.

I now started my fresco act on the walls of the Douve farm.

I spent most of the day on the job, and discovered how some startling effects could be produced.

Materials were: A bottle of Indian ink, a couple of brushes, about a hundredweight of useless charcoal, and a G.S. blue and red pencil.

Amongst the rough sketches that I did that day were the original drawings for two subsequent "Fragments" of mine.

One was the rough idea for "They've evidently seen me," and the other was "My dream for years to come." The idea for "They've evidently seen me" came whilst carrying back that table to St. Yvon, as I mentioned in a previous chapter, but the scenario for the idea was not provided for until I went to this farm some time later. In intervals of working at the walls I rambled about the farm building, and went up into a loft over a barn at the end of the farm nearest the trenches. I looked out through a hole in the tiles just in time to hear a shell come over from away back amongst the Germans somewhere, and land about five hundred yards to the left. The sentence, "They've evidently seen me," came flashing across my mind again, and I now saw the correct setting in my mind: *i.e.*, the enthusiastic observer looking out of the top of a narrow chimney, whilst a remarkably well-aimed shell leads "him of the binoculars" to suppose that they *have* seen him.

I came downstairs and made a pencil sketch of my idea, and before I left the trenches that time I had done a wash drawing and sent it to England. This was my second "Fragment."

The other sketch, "My dream for years to come," was drawn on one wall of a small apple or potato room, opening off our big room, and the drawing occupied the whole wall.

I knocked off drawing about four o'clock, and did a little of the alternative occupation, that of looking out through the cracked windows on to the mutilated courtyard in front. It was getting darker now, and nearing the time when I had to put on all my tackle, and gird myself up for my round of the trenches. As soon as it was nearly dark I started out. The other officers generally left a bit later, but as I had such a long way to go, and as I wanted to examine the country while there was yet a little light, I started at dusk. Not yet knowing exactly how much the enemy could see on the open mud flat, I determined to go along by the river bank, and by keeping among the trees I hoped to escape observation. I made for the Douve, and soon got along as far as the row of farms. I explored all these, and a shocking sight they were. All charred and ruined, and the skeleton remains slowly decomposing away into the unwholesome ground about them. I went inside several of the dismantled rooms. Nearly all contained old and battered bits of soldiers' equipment, empty tins, and remnants of Belgian property. Sad relics of former billeting: a living reminder of the rough times that had preceded our arrival in this locality. I passed on to another farm, and entered the yard near the river. It was nearly full of black wooden crosses, roughly made and painted over with tar. All that was left to mark the graves of those who had died to get our trenches where they were—at the bottom of the Messines ridge. A bleak and sombre winter's night, that courtyard of the ruined farm, the rows of crosses—I often think of it all now.

As the darkness came on I proceeded towards the trenches, and when it had become sufficiently dark I entered the old farm by the reserve trench and crossed the yard to enter the field which led to the first of our trenches. At St. Yvon it was pretty airy work, going the rounds at night, but this was a jolly sight more so. The country was far more open, and although the Boches couldn't see us, yet they kept up an incessant sniping demonstration. Picking up my sergeant at Number 1 trench, he and I started on our tour.

We made a long and exhaustive examination that night, both of the existing machine-gun emplacements and of the entire ground, with a view to changing our positions. It was a long time before I finally left the trenches and started off across the desolate expanse to the Douve farm, and I was dead beat when I arrived there. On getting into the big room I found the Colonel, who had just come in. "Where's that right-hand gun of yours, Bairnsfather?" he asked. "Down on the right of Number 2 trench, sir," I answered; "just by the two willows near the sap which runs out towards Number 1." "It's not much of a place for it," he said; "where we ought to have it is to the right of the sap, so that it enfilades the whole front of that trench." "When do you want it moved, sir?" I asked. "Well, it ought to be done at once; it's no good where it is."

That fixed it. I knew what he wanted; so I started out again, back over the mile and a half to alter the gun. It was a weary job; but I would have gone on going back and altering the whole lot for our Colonel, who was the best line in commanding officers I ever struck. Every one had the most perfect confidence in him. He was the most shell, bullet, and bomb defying person I have ever seen. When I got back for the second time that night I was quite ready to roll up in the straw, and be lulled off to sleep by the cracking rifle fire outside.

CHAPTER XIX

VISIONS OF LEAVE—
DICK TURPIN—LEAVE!

Our first time in the Douve trenches was mainly uneventful, but we all decided it was not as pleasant as St. Yvon. For my part, it was fifty per cent. worse than St. Yvon; but I was now buoyed up by a new light in the sky, which made the first time in more tolerable than it might otherwise have been. It was getting near my turn for leave! I had been looking forward to this for a long time, but there were many who had to take their turn in front of me, so I had dismissed the case for a bit. Recently, however, the powers that be had been sending more than one officer away at a time; consequently my turn was rapidly approaching. We came away back to billets in the usual way after our first dose of the Douve, and all wallowed off to our various billeting quarters. I was hot and strong on the leave idea now. It was really getting close and I felt disposed to find everything *couleur de rose*. Even the manure heap in the billeting farm yard looked covered with roses. I could have thrown a bag of confetti at the farmer's wife—it's most exhilarating to think of the coming of one's first leave. One maps out what one will do with the time in a hundred different ways. I was wondering how I could manage to transport my souvenirs home, as I had collected a pretty good supply by this time—shell cases, fuse tops, clogs, and that Boche rifle I got on Christmas Day.

One morning (we had been about two days out) I got a note from the Adjutant to say I could put in my application. I put it in all right and then sat down and hoped for the best.

My spirits were now raised to such a pitch that I again decided to ride to Nieppe—just for fun.

I rode away down the long winding line, smiling at everything on either side—the three-sailed windmill with the top off; the estaminet with the hole through the gable end—all objects seemed to radiate peace and goodwill. There was a very bright sun in the sky that day. I rode down to the high road, and cantered along the grass at the side into Nieppe. Just as I entered the town I met a friend riding out. He shouted something at me. I couldn't hear what he said. "What?" I yelled.

"All leave's cancelled!"

That was enough for me. I rode into Nieppe like an infuriated cowboy. I went straight for the divisional headquarters, flung away the horse and dashed up into the building. I knew one or two of the officers there. "What's this about leave?" I asked. "All about to be cancelled," was the reply. "If you're quick, you may get yours through, as you've been out here long enough, and you're next to go." "What have I got to do?" I screamed. "Go to your Colonel, and ask him to wire the Corps headquarters and ask them to let you go; only you'll have to look sharp about it."

He needn't have told me that. He had hardly finished before I was outside and making for my horse. I got out of Nieppe as quickly as I could, and lit out for our battalion headquarters. About four miles to go, but I lost no time about it. "Leave cancelled!" I hissed through the triangular gap in my front tooth, as I galloped along the road; "leave cancelled!"

I should have made a good film actor that day: "Dick Turpin's ride to York" in two reels. I reached the turning off the high road all right, and pursued my wild career down the lanes which led to the Colonel's headquarters. The road wound about in a most ridiculous way, making salients out of ploughed fields on either side. I decided to throw all prudence to the winds, and cut across these. My horse evidently thought this an excellent idea, for as soon as he got on the fields he was off like a trout up stream. Most successful across the first salient, then, suddenly, I saw we were approaching a wide ditch. Leave *would* be cancelled as far as I was concerned if I tried to jump that, I felt certain. I saw a sort of a narrow bridge about fifty yards to the right. Tried to persuade the horse to make for it. No, he believed in the ditch idea, and put on a sprint to jump it. Terrific battle between Dick Turpin and Black Bess!

A foaming pause on the brink of the abyss. Dick Turpin wins the argument, and after a few prancing circles described in the field manages to cross the bridge with his fiery steed. I then rode down the road into the little village. The village school had been turned into a battalion stores, and the quartermaster-sergeant was invariably to be found there. I dismounted and pulled my horse up a couple of steps into the large schoolroom. Tied him up here, and last saw him blowing clouds of steam out of his nose on to one of those maps which show interesting forms of vegetable life with their Latin names underneath. Now for the Colonel. I clattered off down the street to his temporary orderly room. Thank heaven, he was in! I explained the case to him. He said he would do his best, and there and then sent off a wire. I could do no more now, so after fixing up that a message should be sent me, I slowly retraced my steps to the school, extracted the horse, and wended my way slowly back to the Transport Farm. Here I languished for the rest of the day, feeling convinced that "all leave was cancelled." I sat down to do some sketching after tea, full of marmalade and depression. About 6 p.m. I chucked it, and went and sat by the stove, smoking a pipe. Suddenly the door opened and a bicycle orderly came in: "There's a note from the Adjutant for you, sir."

I tore it open. "Your leave granted; you leave to-morrow. If you call here in the morning, I'll give you your pass."

LEAVE!!

CHAPTER XX

THAT LEAVE TRAIN—MY OLD PAL— LONDON AND HOME—THE CALL OF THE WILD

One wants to have been at the front, in the nasty parts, to appreciate fully what getting seven days' leave feels like. We used to have to be out at the front for three consecutive months before being entitled to this privilege. I had passed this necessary apprenticeship, and now had actually got my leave.

The morning after getting my instructions I rose early, and packed the few things I was going to take with me. Very few things they were, too. Only a pack and a haversack, and both contained nothing but souvenirs. I decided to go to the station via the orderly room, so that I could do both in one journey. I had about two miles to go from my billets to the orderly room in the village, and about a mile on from there to the station. Some one suggested my riding—no fear; I was running no risks now. I started off early with my servant. We took it in shifts with my heavy bags of souvenirs. One package (the pack) had four "Little Willie" cases inside, in other words, the cast-iron shell cases for the German equivalent of our 18-pounders. The haversack was filled with aluminium fuse tops and one large piece of a "Jack Johnson" shell case. My pockets—and I had a good number, as I was wearing my greatcoat—were filled with a variety of objects. A pair of little clogs found in a roof at St. Yvon, several clips of German bullets removed from equipment found on Christmas Day, and a collection of bullets which I had picked out with my pocket knife from the walls of our house in St. Yvon. The only additional luggage to this inventory I have given was my usual copious supply of Gold Flake cigarettes, of which, during my life in France, I must have consumed several army corps.

It was a glorious day—bright, sunny, and a faint fresh wind. Everything seemed bright and rosy. I felt I should have liked to skip along the road like a young bay tree—no, that's wrong—like a ram, only I didn't think it would be quite the thing with my servant there (King's Regulations: Chapter 158, paragraph 96, line 4); besides, he wasn't going on leave, so it would have been rather a dirty trick after all.

We got to the village with aching arms and souvenirs intact. I got my pass, and together with another officer we set out for the station. It was a leave train. Officers from all sorts of different battalions were either in it or going to get in, either here or at the next stop.

Having no wish to get that station into trouble, or myself either, by mentioning its name, I will call it Crême de Menthe. It was the same rotten little place I had arrived at. It is only because I am trying to sell the "station-master" a copy of this book that I call the place a station at all. It really is a decomposing collection of half-hearted buildings and moss-grown rails, with an apology for a platform at one side.

We caught the train with an hour to spare. You can't miss trains in France: there's too much margin allowed on the time-table. The 10.15 leaves at 11.30, the 11.45 at 2.20, and so on; besides, if you did miss your train, you could always catch it up about two fields away, so there's nothing to worry about.

We started. I don't know what time it was.

If you turn up the word "locomotion" in a dictionary, you will find it means "the act or power of moving from place to place"; from *locus*, a place, and *motion*, the act of moving. Our engine had got the *locus* part all right, but was rather weak about the *motion*. We creaked and squeaked about up the moss-grown track, and groaned our way back into the station time after time, in order to tie on something else behind the train, or to get on to a siding to let a trainload of trench floorboards and plum and apple jangle past up the line. When at last we really started, it was about at the speed of the "Rocket" on its trial trip.

Our enthusiastic "going on leave" ardour was severely tested, and nearly broke down before we reached Boulogne, which we did late that night. But getting there, and mingling with the leave-going crowd which thronged the buffet, made up for all travelling shortcomings. Every variety of officer and army official was represented there. There were colonels, majors, captains, lieutenants, quantities of private soldiers, sergeants and corporals, hospital nurses and various other people employed in some war capacity or other. Representatives from every branch of the Army, in fact, whose turn for leave had come.

I left the buffet for a moment to go across to the Transport Office, and walking along through the throng ran into my greatest friend. A most extraordinary chance this! I had not the least idea whereabouts in France he was, or when he might be likely to get leave. His job was in quite a different part, many miles from the Douve. I have known him for many years; we were at school together, and have always seemed to have the lucky knack of bobbing up to the surface simultaneously without prior arrangement. This meeting sent my spirits up higher than ever. We both adjourned to the buffet, and talked away about our various experiences to the accompaniment of cold chicken and ham. A merry scene truly, that buffet—every one filled with thoughts of England. Nearly every one there must have stepped out of the same sort of mud and danger bath that I had. And, my word! it is a first-class feeling: sitting about waiting for the boat when you feel you've earned this seven days' leave. You hear men on all sides getting the last ounce of appreciation out of the unique sensation by saying such things as, "Fancy those poor blighters, sitting in the mud up there; they'll be just about getting near 'Stand to' now."

You rapidly dismiss a momentary flash in your mind of what it's going to be like in that buffet on the return journey.

Early in the morning, and while it was still dark, we left the harbour and ploughed out into the darkness and the sea towards England.

I claim the honoured position of the world's worst sailor. I have covered several thousand miles on the sea, "brooked the briny" as far as India and Canada. I have been hurtled about on the largest Atlantic waves; yet I am, and always will remain, absolutely impossible at sea. Looking at the docks out of the hotel window nearly sends me to bed; there's something about a ship that takes the stuffing out of me completely. Whether it's that horrible pale varnished woodwork, mingled with the smell of stuffy upholstery, or whether it's that nauseating whiff from the open hatch of the engine-room, I don't know; but once on a ship I am as naught . . . not nautical.

Of course the Channel was going to be rough. I could see that at a glance. I know exactly what to do about the sea now. I go straight to a bunk, and hope for the best; if no bunk—bribe the steward until there is one.

I got a bunk, deserted my friend in a cheerless way, and retired till the crossing was over. It *was* very rough . . .

In the cold grey hours we glided into Dover or Folkestone (I was too anaemic to care which) and fastened up alongside the wharf. I had a dim recollection of getting my pal to hold my pack as we left Boulogne, and now I could see neither him nor the pack. Fearful crush struggling up the gangway. I had to scramble for a seat in the London train, so couldn't waste time looking for my friend. I had my haversack—he had my pack.

The train moved off, and now here we all were back in clean, fresh, luxurious England, gliding along in an English train towards London. It's worth doing months and months of trenches to get that buoyant, electrical sensation of passing along through English country on one's way to London on leave.

I spent the train journey thinking over what I should do during my seven days. Time after time I mentally conjured up the forthcoming performance of catching the train at Paddington and gliding out of the shadows of the huge station into the sunlit country beyond—the rapid express journey down home, the drive out from the station, back in my own land again!

We got into London in pretty quick time, and I rapidly converted my dreams into facts.

Still in the same old trench clothes, with a goodly quantity of Flanders mud attached, I walked into Paddington station, and collared a seat in the train on Number 1 platform. Then, collecting a quantity of papers and magazines from the bookstalls, I prepared myself for enjoying to the full the two hours' journey down home.

I spent a gorgeous week in Warwickshire, during which time my friend came along down to stay a couple of days with me, bringing my missing pack along with him. He had had the joy of carrying it laden with shell cases across London, and taking it down with him to somewhere near Aldershot, and finally bringing it to me without having kept any of the contents . . . Such is a true friend.

As this book deals with my wanderings in France I will not go into details of my happy seven days' leave. I now resume at the point where I was due to return to France. In spite of the joys of England as opposed to life in Flanders, yet a curious phenomenon presented itself at the end of my leave. I was anxious to get back. Strange, but true. Somehow one felt that slogging away out in the dismal fields of war was the real thing to do. If some one had offered me a nice, safe, comfortable job in England, I wouldn't have taken it. I claim no credit for this feeling of mine. I know every one has the same. That buccaneering, rough and tumble life out there has its attractions. The spirit of adventure is in most people, and the desire and will to biff the Boches is in every one, so there you are.

I drifted back via London, Dover and Boulogne, and thence up the same old stagnant line to Crême de Menthe. Once more back in the land of mud, bullets, billets, and star shells.

It was the greyest of grey days when I arrived at my one-horse terminus. I got out at the "station," and had a solitary walk along the empty, muddy lanes, back to the Transport Farm.

Plodding along in the thin rain that was falling I thought of home, London, England, and then of the job before me. Another three months at least before any further chance of leave could come my way again. Evening was coming on. Across the flat, sombre country I could see the tall, swaying poplar trees standing near the farm. Beyond lay the rough and rugged road which led to the Douve trenches.

How nice that leave had been! To-morrow night I should be going along back to the trenches before Wulverghem.

CHAPTER XXI

BACK FROM LEAVE—THAT "BLINKIN' MOON" —JOHNSON 'OLES— TOMMY AND "FRIGHTFULNESS" — EXPLORING EXPEDITION

As I had expected, the battalion were just finishing their last days out in rest billets, and were going "in" the following night.

Reaction from leave set in for me with unprecedented violence. It was horrible weather, pouring with rain all the time, which made one's depression worse.

Leave over; rain, rain, rain; trenches again, and the future looked like being perpetually the same, or perhaps worse. Yet, somehow or other, in these times of deep depression which come to every one now and again, I cannot help smiling. It has always struck me as an amusing thing that the world, and all the human beings thereon, do get themselves into such curious and painful predicaments, and then spend the rest of the time wishing they could get out.

My reflections invariably brought me to the same conclusion, that here I was, caught up in the cogs of this immense, uncontrollable war machine, and like every one else, had to, and meant to stick it out to the end.

The next night we went through all the approved formula for going into the trenches. Started at dusk, and got into our respective mud cavities a few hours later. I went all round the trenches again, looking to see that things were the same as when I left them, and, on the Colonel's instructions, started a series of alterations in several gun positions. There was one trench that was so obscured along its front by odd stumps of trees that I decided the only good spot for a machine gun was right at one end, on a road which led up to Messines. From here it would be possible for us to get an excellent field of fire. To have this gun on the road meant making an emplacement there somehow. That night we started scheming it out, and the next evening began work on it. It was a bright moonlight night, I remember, and my sergeant and I went out in front of our parapet, walked along the field and crept up the ditch a little way, considering the machine-gun possibilities of the land. That moonlight feeling is very curious. You feel as if the enemy can see you clearly, and that all eyes in the opposite trench are turned on you. You can almost imagine a Boche smilingly taking an aim, and saying to a friend, "We'll just let him come a bit closer first." Every one who has had to go "out in front," wiring, will know this feeling. As a matter of fact, it is astonishing how little one can see of men in the moonlight, even when the trenches are very close together. One gets quite used to walking about freely in this light, going out in front of the parapet and having a look round. The only time that really makes one apprehensive is when some gang of men or other turn up from way back somewhere, and have come to assist in some operation near the enemy. They, being unfamiliar with the caution needed, and unappreciative of what it's like to have neighbours who "hate" you sixty yards away, generally bring trouble in their wake by one of the party shouting out in a deep bass or a shrill soprano, "'Ere, chuck us the 'ammer, 'Arry," or something like that, following the remark up with a series of vulcan-like blows on the top of an iron post. Result: three star shells soar out into the frosty air, and a burst of machine-gun fire skims over the top of your head.

We made a very excellent and strong emplacement on the road, and used it henceforth. I had a lot of bother with one gun in those trenches, which was placed at very nearly the left-hand end of the whole line. I had been obliged to fix the gun there, as it was very necessary for dominating a certain road. But when I took the place over from the previous battalion, I thought there might be difficulties about this gun position, and there were. The night before we had made our inspection of these trenches, a shell had landed right on top of the gun emplacement and had "outed" the whole concern, unfortunately killing two of the gun

All round that neighbourhood it seemed to have been the fashion, past and present, to use the largest shells. In going along the Douve one day, I made a point of measuring and examining several of the holes. I took a photograph of one, with my cap resting on one side of it, to show the relative proportion and give an idea of the size. It was about fourteen feet in diameter, and seven feet deep. The largest shell hole I have ever seen was over twenty feet in diameter and about twelve feet deep. The largest hole I have seen, made by an implement of war, though not by a gun or a howitzer, was larger still, and its size was colossal. I refer to a hole made by one of our trench mortars, but regret that I did not measure it. Round about our farm were a series of holes of immense size, showing clearly the odium which that farm had incurred, and was incurring; but, whilst I was in it, nothing came in through the roof or walls. I have since learnt that that old farm is no more, having been shelled out of existence. All my sketches on those plaster walls form part of a slack heap, surrounded by a moat.

Well, this persistent shelling of the left-hand end of our trenches meant a persistent readjustment of our parapets, and putting things back again. Each morning the Boches would knock things down, and each evening we would put them up again. Our soldiers are only amused by this procedure. Their humorously cynical outlook at the Boche temper renders them impervious to anything the Germans can ever do or think of. Their outlook towards a venomous German attempt to do something "frightfully" nasty, is very similar to a large and powerful nurse dealing with a fractious child—sort of: "Now, then, Master Frankie, you mustn't kick and scream like that."

One can almost see a group of stolid, unimaginative, non-humorous Germans, taking all things with their ridiculous seriousness, sending off their shells, and pulling hateful faces at the same time. You can see our men sending over a real stiff, quietening answer, with a sporting twinkle in the eye, perhaps jokingly remarking, as a shell is pushed into the gun, "'Ere's one for their Officers' Mess, Bert."

On several evenings I had to go round and arrange for the reconstruction of the ruined parapet or squashed-in dug-outs. It was during one of these little episodes that I felt the spirit of my drawing, "There goes our blinking parapet again," which I did sometime later. I never went about looking for ideas for drawings; the whole business of the war seemed to come before me in a series of pictures. Jokes used to stick out of all the horrible discomfort, something like the points of a harrow would stick into you if you slept on it.

I used to visit all the trenches, and look up the various company commanders and platoon commanders in the same way as I did at St. Yvon. I got a splendid idea of all the details of our position; all the various ways from one part of it to another. As I walked back to the Douve farm at night, nearly always alone, I used to keep on exploring the wide tract of land that lay behind our trenches. "I'll have a look at that old cottage up on the right to-night," I used to say to myself, and later, when the time came for me to walk back from the trenches, I would go off at a new angle across the plain, and make for my objective. Once inside, and feeling out of view of the enemy, I would go round the deserted rooms and lofts by the light of a few matches, and if the house looked as if it would prove of interest, I would return the next night with a candle-end, and make an examination of the whole thing. They are all very much alike, these houses in Flanders; all seem to contain the same mangled remains of simple, homely occupations. Strings of onions, old straw hats, and clogs, mixed with an assortment of cheap clothing, with perhaps here and there an umbrella or a top hat. That is about the class of stuff one found in them. After one of these expeditions I would go on back across the plain, along the corduroy boards or by the bank of the river, to our farm.

CHAPTER XXII

A DAYLIGHT STALK—THE DISUSED TRENCH—"DID THEY SEE ME?"— A GOOD SNIPING POSITION

Our farm was, as I have remarked, a mile from the trenches at the nearest part, and about a mile and a half from the furthest. Wulverghem was about half a mile behind the farm.

As time went on at these Douve trenches, I became more and more familiar with the details of the surrounding country, for each day I used to creep out of the farm, and when I had crossed the moat by a small wooden bridge at the back, I would go off into the country near by looking at everything. One day the Colonel expressed a wish to know whether it was possible to get up into our trenches in day time without being seen. Of course any one could have gone to the trenches, and been momentarily seen here and there, and could have done so fairly safely and easily by simply walking straight up, taking advantage of what little cover there was; but to get right up without showing at all, was rather a poser, as all cover ceased about a hundred yards behind the trenches.

The idea of trying attracted me. One morning I crept along the ragged hedge, on the far side of the moat which led to the river, and started out for the trenches. I imagined a German with a powerful pair of binoculars looking down on the plain from the Messines Hill, with nothing better to do than to see if he could spot some one walking about. Keeping this possibility well in mind, I started my stalk up to the trenches with every precaution.

I crept along amongst the trees bordering the river for a considerable distance, but as one neared the trenches, these got wider apart, and as the river wound about a lot there were places where to walk from one tree to the next, one had to walk parallel to the German trenches and quite exposed, though, of course, at a considerable range off. I still bore in mind my imaginary picture of the gentleman with binoculars, though, so I got down near the water's edge and moved along, half-concealed by the bank. Soon I reached the farms, and by dodging about amongst the scattered shrubs and out-houses, here and there crawling up a ditch, I got into one of the farm buildings. I sat in it amongst a pile of old clothes, empty tins and other oddments, and had a smoke, thinking the while on how I could get from these farms across the last bit of open space which was the most difficult of all.

I finished my cigarette, and began the stalk again. Another difficulty presented itself. I found that it was extremely difficult to cross from the second last farm to the last one, as the ground was completely open, and rather sloped down towards the enemy. This was not apparent when looking at the place at night, for then one never bothers about concealment, and one walks anywhere and anyhow. But now the question was, how to do it. I crept down to the river again, and went along there for a bit, looking for a chance of leaving it under cover for the farm.

Coming to a narrow, cart-rutted lane a little further on, I was just starting to go up it when, suddenly, a bright idea struck me. An old zig-zag communication trench (a relic of a bygone period) left the lane on the right, and apparently ran out across the field to within a few yards of the furthest farm. Once there, I had only a hundred yards more to do.

I entered the communication trench. It was just a deep, narrow slot cut across the field, and had, I should imagine, never been used. I think the enormous amount of water in it had made it a useless work. I saw no sign of it ever having been used. A fearful trench it was, with a deep deposit of dark green filthy, watery mud from end to end.

131

This, I could see, was the only way up to the farm, so I made the best of it. I resigned myself to getting thoroughly wet through. Quite unavoidable. I plunged into this unwholesome clay ditch and went along, each step taking me up to my thighs in soft dark ooze, whilst here and there the water was so deep as to force me to scoop out holes in the clay at the side when, by leaning against the opposite side, with my feet in the holes, I could slowly push my way along. In time I got to the other end, and sat down to think a bit. As I sat, a bullet suddenly whacked into the clay parapet alongside of me, which stimulated my thinking a bit. "Had I been seen?" I tried to find out, and reassure myself before going on. I put my hat on top of a stick and brought it up above the parapet at two or three points to try and attract another shot; but no, there wasn't another, so I concluded the first one had been accidental, and went on my way again. By wriggling along behind an undulation in the field, and then creeping from one tree to another, I at last managed to get up into our reserve trenches, where I obtained my first daylight, close-up view of our trenches, German trenches, and general landscape; all laid out in panorama style.

In front of me were our front-line trenches, following the line of the little stream which ran into the Douve on the right. On the far side of the stream the ground gently rose in a long slope up to Messines, where you could see a shattered mass of red brick buildings with the old grey tower in the middle. At a distance of from about two to four hundred yards away lay the German trenches, parallel to ours, their barbed wire glistening in the morning sunlight.

"This place I'm in is a pretty good place for a sniper to hitch up," I thought to myself. "Can see everything there is to be seen from here."

After a short stocktaking of the whole scene, I turned and wallowed my way back to the farm. Some few days later they did make a sniper's post of that spot, and a captain friend of mine, with whom I spent many quaint and dismal nights in St. Yvon, occupied it. He was the "star" shot of the battalion, an expert sniper, and, I believe, made quite a good bag.

CHAPTER XXIII

OUR MOATED FARM—WULVERGHEM—
THE CURÉ'S HOUSE—A SHATTERED
CHURCH —MORE "HEAVIES"—A FARM
ON FIRE

Our farm was one of a cluster of three or four, each approximately a couple of hundred yards apart. It was perhaps the largest and the most preserved of the lot. It was just the same sort of shape as all Flemish farms—a long building running round three sides of the yard, in the middle of which there was an oblong tank, used for collecting all the rubbish and drainage.

The only difference about our farm was, we had a moat. Very superior to all the cluster in consequence. Sometime or other the moat must have been very effective; but when I was there, only about a quarter of it contained water. The other three-quarters was a sort of bog, or marsh, its surface broken up by large shell holes. On the driest part of this I discovered a row of graves, their rough crosses all battered and bent down. I just managed to discern the names inscribed; they were all French. Names of former heroes who had participated in some action or other months before. Going out into the fields behind the farm, I found more French graves, enclosed in a rectangular graveyard that had been roughly made with barbed wire and posts, each grave surmounted with the dead soldier's hat. Months of rough wintry weather had beaten down the faded cloth cap into the clay mound, and had started the obliteration of the lettering on the cross. A few more months; and cross, mound and hat will all have merged back into the fields of Flanders.

Beyond these fields, about half a mile distant, lay Wulverghem. Looking at what you can see of this village from the Douve farm, it looks exceedingly pretty and attractive. A splendid old church tower could be seen between the trees, and round about it were clustered the red roofs of a fair-sized village. It has, to my mind, a very nice situation. In the days before the war it must have been a pleasing place to live in. I went to have a look at it one day. It's about as fine a sample of what these Prussians have brought upon Belgian villages as any I have seen. The village street is one long ruin. On either side of the road, all the houses are merely a collection of broken tiles and shattered bricks and framework. Huge shell holes punctuate the street. I had seen a good many mutilated villages before this, but I remember thinking this was as bad, if not worse, than any I had yet seen. I determined to explore some of the houses and the church.

I went into one house opposite the church. It had been quite a nice house once, containing about ten rooms. It was full of all sorts of things. The evacuation had evidently been hurried. I went into the front right-hand room first, and soon discovered by the books and pictures that this had been the Curé's house. It was in a terrible state. Religious books in French and Latin lay about the floor in a vast disorder, some with the cover and half the book torn off by the effect of an explosion. Pictures illustrating Bible scenes, images, and other probably cherished objects, smashed and ruined, hung about the walls, or fragmentary portions of them lay littered about on the floor.

A shell hole of large proportions had rent a gash in the outer front wall, leaving the window woodwork, bricks and wall-paper piled up in a heap on the floor, partially obliterating a large writing desk. Private papers lay about in profusion, all dirty, damp and muddy. The remains of a window blind and half its roller hung in the space left by the absent window, and mournfully tapped against the remnant of the framework in the light, cold breeze that was blowing in from outside. Place this scene in your imagination in some luxuriant country vicarage in England, and you will get an idea of what Belgium has had to put up with from these Teutonic madmen. I went into all the rooms; they were in very much the same state. In the back part of the house the litter was added to by empty tins and old military equipment. Soldiers had evidently had to live there temporarily on their way to some part of our lines. I heard a movement in the room opposite the one I had first gone into; I went back and saw a cat sitting in the corner amongst a pile of leather-backed books. I made a movement towards it, but with a cadaverous, wild glare at me, it sprang through the broken window and disappeared.

The church was just opposite the priest's house. I went across the road to look at it. It was a large reddish-grey stone building, pretty old, I should say, and surrounded by a graveyard. Shell holes everywhere; the old, grey grave stones and slabs cracked and sticking about at odd angles. As I entered by the vestry door I noticed the tower was fairly all right, but that was about the only part that was. Belgium and Northern France are full of churches which have been sadly knocked about, and all present very much the same appearance. I will describe this one to give you a sample. I went through the vestry into the main part of the church, deciding to examine the vestry later. The roof had had most of the tiles blown off, and underneath them the roofing-boards had been shattered into long narrow strips. Fixed at one end to what was left of the rafters they flapped slowly up and down in the air like lengths of watch-spring. Below, on the floor of the church, the chairs were tossed about in the greatest possible disorder, and here and there a dozen or so had been pulverized by the fall of an immense block of masonry. Highly coloured images were lying about, broken and twisted. The altar candelabra and stained-glass windows lay in a heap together behind a pulpit, the front of which had been knocked off by a falling pillar. One could walk about near some of

135

the broken images, and pick up little candles and trinkets which had been put in and around the shrine, off the floor and from among the mass of broken stones and mortar. The vestry, I found, was almost complete. Nearly trodden out of recognition on the floor, I found a bright coloured hand-made altar cloth, which I then had half a mind to take away with me, and post it back to some parson in England to put in his church. I only refrained from carrying out this plan as I feared that the difficulties of getting it away would be too great. I left the church, and looked about some of the other houses, but none proved as pathetically interesting as the church and the vicar's house, so I took my way out across the fields again towards the Douve farm.

Not a soul about anywhere. Wulverghem lay there, empty, wrecked and deserted. I walked along the river bank for a bit, and had got about two hundred yards from the farm when the quiet morning was interrupted in the usual way, by shelling. Deep-toned, earth-shaking crashes broke into the quiet peaceful air. "Just in the same place," I observed to myself as I walked along behind our left-hand trenches. I could see the cloud of black smoke after each one landed, and knew exactly where they were. "Just in the same old—hullo! hullo!" With that rotating, gurgling whistle a big one had just sailed over and landed about fifty yards from our farm! I nipped in across the moat, through the courtyard, and explained to the others where it had landed. We all remained silent, waiting for the next. Here it came, gurgling along through the air; a pause, then "Crumph!"—nearly in the same place again, but, if anything, nearer the next farm. The Colonel moved to the window and looked out. "They're after that farm," he said, as he turned away slowly and struck a match by the fireplace to light his pipe with. About half a dozen shells whizzed along in close succession, and about four hit and went into the roof of the next farm.

Presently I looked out of the window again, and saw a lot of our men moving out of the farm and across the road into the field beyond. There was a reserve trench here, so they went into it. I looked again, and soon saw the reason. Dense columns of smoke were coming out of the straw roof, and soon the whole place was a blazing ruin. Nobody in the least perturbed; we all turned away from the window and wondered how soon they'd "have our farm."

CHAPTER XXIV

THAT RATION FATIGUE—SKETCHES IN REQUEST—BAILLEUL—BATHS AND LUNATICS—HOW TO CONDUCT A WAR

They seemed to me long, dark, dismal days, those days spent in the Douve trenches; longer, darker and more dismal than the Plugstreet ones. Night after night I crossed the dreary mud flat, passed the same old wretched farms, and went on with the same old trench routine. We all considered the trenches a pretty rotten outfit; but every one was fully prepared to accept far rottener things than that. There was never the least sign of flagging determination in any man there, and I am sure you could say the same of the whole front.

And, really, some jobs on some nights wanted a lot of beating for undesirability. Take the ration party's job, for instance. Think of the rottenest, wettest, windiest winter's night you can remember, and add to it this bleak, muddy, war-worn plain with its ruined farms and shell-torn lonely road. Then think of men, leaving the trenches at dusk, going back about a mile and a half, and bringing sundry large and heavy boxes up to the trenches, pausing now and again for a rest, and ignoring the intermittent crackling of rifle fire in the darkness, and the sharp "*phit*" of bullets hitting the mud all around. Think of that as your portion each night and every night. When you have finished this job, the rest you get consists of coiling yourself up in a damp dug-out. Night after night, week after week, month after month, this job is done by thousands. As one sits in a brilliantly illuminated, comfortable, warm theatre, having just come from a cosy and luxurious restaurant, just think of some poor devil half-way along those corduroy boards struggling with a crate of biscuits; the ration "dump" behind, the trenches on in front. When he has finished he will step down into the muddy slush of a trench, and take his place with the rest, who, if need be, will go on doing that job for another ten years, without thinking of an alternative. The Germans made a vast mistake when they thought they had gauged the English temperament.

* * * * *

We went "in" and "out" of those trenches many times. During these intervals of "out" I began to draw pictures more and more. It had become known that I drew these trench pictures, not only in our battalion but in several others, and at various headquarters I got requests for four or five drawings at a time. About three weeks after I returned from leave, I had to move my billeting quarters. I went to a farm called "La petite Monque"; I don't know how it's really spelt, but that's what the name sounded like. Here I lived with the officers of A Company, and a jolly pleasant crew they were. We shared a mess together, and had one big room and one small room between us. There were six of us altogether. The Captain had the little room and the bed in it, whilst we all slept round the table on the floor in the big room. Here, in the daytime, when I was not out with the machine-gun sections, I drew several pictures. The Brigadier-General of our brigade took a particular fancy to one which he got from me. The divisional headquarters had half a dozen; whilst I did two sets of four each for two officers in the regiment.

Sometimes we would go for walks around the country, and occasionally made an excursion as far as Bailleul, about five miles away. Bailleul held one special attraction for us. There were some wonderfully good baths there. The fact that they were situated in the lunatic asylum rather added to their interest.

"I hear you Callin' me

The first time I went there, one of the subalterns in A Company was my companion. We didn't particularly want to walk all the way, so we decided to get down to the high road as soon as we could, and try and get a lift in a car. With great luck we managed to stop a fairly empty car, and got a lift. It was occupied by a couple of French soldiers who willingly rolled us along into Bailleul. Once there, we walked through the town and out to the asylum close by. I expect by now the lunatics have been called up under the group system; but in those days they were there, and pulled faces at us as we walked up the wide gravel drive to the grand portals of the building. They do make nice asylums over there. This was a sort of Chatsworth or Blenheim to look at. Inside it was fitted up in very great style: long carpeted corridors opening out into sort of domed winter gardens, something like the snake house at the Zoo. We came at length to a particularly lofty, domed hall, from which opened several large bathrooms. Splendid places. A row of large white enamelled baths along one wall, cork mats on the floor, and one enormous central water supply, hot and cold, which you diverted to whichever bath you chose by means of a long flexible rubber pipe. Soap, sponges, towels, *ad lib*. You can imagine what this palatial water grotto meant to us, when, at other times, our best bath was of saucepan capacity, taken on the cold stone floor of a farm room. We lay and boiled the trenches out of our systems in that palatial asylum. Glorious! lying back in a long white enamel bath in a warm foggy atmosphere of steam, watching one's toes floating in front. When this was over, and we had been grimaced off the premises by "inmates" at the windows, we went back into Bailleul and made for the "Faucon d'Or," an old hotel that stands in the square. Here we had a civilized meal. Tablecloth, knives, forks, spoons, waited on, all that sort of thing. You could have quite a good dinner here if you liked. A curious thought occurred to me then, and as it occurs again to me now I write it down. Here it is: If the authorities gave one permission, one could have rooms at the Faucon d'Or and go to the war daily. It would be quite possible to, say, have an early dinner, table d'hote (with, say, a half-bottle of Salmon and Gluckstein), get into one's car and go to the trenches, spend the night sitting in a small damp hole in the ground, or glaring over the parapet, and after "stand to" in the morning, go back in the car in time for breakfast. Of course, if there was an attack, the car would have to wait—that's all; and of course you would come to an understanding with the hotel management that the terms were for meals taken in the hotel, and that if you had to remain in the trenches the terms must be reduced accordingly.

A curious war this; you *can* be at a table d'hote dinner, a music-hall entertainment afterwards, and within half an hour be enveloped in the most uncomfortable, soul-destroying trench ever known. I said you can be; I wish I could say you always are.

The last time I was at Bailleul, not many months ago, I heard that we could no longer have baths at the asylum; I don't know why. I think some one told me why, but I can't remember. Whether it was the baths had been shelled, or whether the lunatics objected, it is impossible for me to say; but there's the fact, anyway. "Na Pu" baths at Bailleul.

CHAPTER XXV

GETTING STALE—LONGING FOR CHANGE—WE LEAVE THE DOUVE— ON THE MARCH—SPOTTED FEVER— TEN DAYS' REST

The Douve trenches claimed our battalion for a long time. We went in and out with monotonous regularity, and I went on with my usual work with machine guns. The whole place became more and more depressing to me, and yet, somehow, I have got more ideas for my pictures from this part of the line than any other since or before. One's mental outlook, I find, varies very much from day to day. Some days there were on which I felt quite merry and bright, and strode along on my nightly rambles, calmly ignoring bullets as they whisked about. At other times I felt thoroughly depressed and weary. As time wore on at the Douve, I felt myself getting into a state when it took more and more out of me to keep up my vigour, and suppress my imagination. There were times when I experienced an almost irresistible desire to lie down and sleep during some of my night walks. I would feel an overwhelming desire to ignore the rain and mud, and just coil up in a farm amongst the empty tins and rubbish and sleep, sleep, sleep. I looked forward to sleep to drown out the worries of the daily and nightly life. In fact, I was slowly getting ill, I suppose. The actual rough and ready life didn't trouble me at all. I was bothered with the *idea* of the whole thing. The unnatural atmosphere of things that one likes and looks upon as pleasing, peaceful objects in ordinary times, seemed now to obsess me. It's hard to describe; but the following gives a faint idea of my feelings at this time. Instead of deriving a sense of peace and serenity from picturesque country farms, old trees, setting suns, and singing birds, here was this wretched war business hashing up the whole thing. A farm was a place where you expected a shell through the wall any minute; a tree was the sort of thing the gunners took to range on; a sunset indicated a quantity of light in which it was unsafe to walk abroad. Birds singing were a mockery. All this sort of thing bothered me, and was slowly reducing my physical capacity to "stick it out." But I determined I would stick to the ship, and so I did. The periodical going out to billets and making merry there was a thing to look forward to. Every one comes up in a rebound of spirits on these occasions. In the evenings there, sitting round the table, writing letters, talking, and occasionally having other members of the regiment in to a meal or a call of some sort, made things quite pleasant. There was always the post to look forward to. Quite a thrill went round the room when the door opened and a sergeant came in with an armful of letters and parcels.

Yet during all this latter time at the Douve I longed for a change in trench life. Some activity, some march to somewhere or other; anything to smash up the everlasting stagnant appearance of life there. Suddenly the change came. We were told we had to go out a day before one of our usual sessions in the trenches was ended. We were all immensely pleased. We didn't know where we were bound for, but, anyway, we were going. This news revived me enormously, and everything looked brighter. The departure-night came, and company by company we handed over to a battalion that had come to relieve us, and collected on the road leading back to Neuve Eglise. I handed over all my gun emplacements to the incoming machine-gun officer, and finally collected my various sections with all their tackle on the road as well. We merely marched back to our usual billets that night, but next morning had orders to get all our baggage ready for the transport wagons. We didn't know where we were going, but at about eleven o'clock in the morning we started off on the march, and soon realized that our direction was Bailleul.

On a fine, clear, warm spring day we marched along, all in the best of spirits, songs of all sorts being sung one after the other. As I marched along in the rear of the battalion, at the head of my machine-gun section, I selected items from their repertoire and had them sung "by request." I had some astonishingly fine mouth-organists in my section. When we had "In the trail of the Lonesome Pine" sung by half the section, with mouth-organ accompaniment by the other half, the effect was enormous. We passed several battalions of my regiment on the road, evidently bound for the Armentières direction. Shouts, jokes and much mirth showed the kindred spirits of the passing columns. All battalions of the same regiment, all more or less recruited in the same counties. When we reached Bailleul we halted in the Square, and then I learnt we were to be billeted there. There was apparently some difficulty in getting billets, and so I was faced with the necessity of finding some for my section myself. The transport officer was in the same fix; he wanted a large and commodious farm whenever he hitched up anywhere, as he had a crowd of horses, wagons and men to put up somehow. He and I decided to start out and look for billets on our own.

I found a temporary rest for my section in an old brickyard on the outskirts of the town, and the transport officer and I started out to look for a good farm which we could appropriate.

Bailleul stands on a bit of a hill, so you can get a wide and extensive view of the country from there. We could see several farms perched about in the country. We fixed on the nearest, and walked out to it. No luck; they were willing to have us, but it wasn't big enough. We tried another; same result. I then suggested we should separate, and each try different roads, and thus we should get one quicker. This we did, I going off up a long straight road, and finally coming to a most promising looking edifice on one side—a real large size in farms.

I went into the yard and walked across the dirty cobbles to the front door. The people were most pleasant. I didn't understand a word they said; but when a person pushes a flagon of beer into one of your hands and an apple into the other, one concludes he means to be pleasant, anyway.

I mumbled a lot of jargon to them for some time, and I really believe they saw that I wanted to use their place for a billet. The owner, a man of about forty-five, then started a long and hardy discussion right at me. He put on a serious face at intervals, so I guessed there was something rather important he was trying to convey to me. I was saved from giving my answer by catching sight of my pal, the transport officer, crossing the yard. He came in. "I've brought Jean along to talk," he announced. (Jean was our own battalion interpreter.) "I can't find a place; but this looks all right." Jean and the owner at once dived off into a labyrinth of unintelligible words, from which they emerged five minutes later. We sat around and listened. Jean turned to us and remarked: "They have got fever here, he says, what you call the spotted fever—how you say, spotted fever?—and this farm is out of bounds."

"Oh! spotted fever! I see!" we both said, and slid away out of that farm pretty quick. So that was what that farmer was trying to say to me: spotted fever!

I went down the road wondering whether cerebral meningitis germs preferred apples or beer, or perhaps they liked both; awful thought!

We went back to our original selection and decided to somehow or other squeeze into the farm which we thought too small. Many hours later we got the transport and the machine-gun section fixed up. We spent two nights there. On the second day I went up into Bailleul. Walking along in the Square, looking at the shops and market stalls, I ran into the brigade machine-gun officer.

"Topping about our brigade, isn't it?" he said.

"What's topping?" I asked.

"Why, we're going to have about ten day's rest; we clear off out of here to-morrow to a village about three miles away, and our battalion will billet there. Where we go after that I don't know; but, anyway, ten days' rest. Ten days' rest!!"

"Come and split one at the Faucon d'Or?"

"No thanks, I've just had one."

"Well, come and have another."

CHAPTER XXVI

A PLEASANT CHANGE—
SUZETTE, BERTHE AND MARTHE—
"LA JEUNE FILLE FAROUCHE"—ANDRÉ

On the next morning we left Bailleul, and the whole of our battalion marched off down one of the roads leading out into the country in a westerly direction. The weather was now excellent; so what with a prospect of a rest, fine weather and the departure from the Wulverghem trenches, we were all very merry and bright, and "going strong" all round. It seemed to us as if we had come out of some dark, wet under-world into a bright, wholesome locality, suitable for the habitation of man.

Down the long, straight, dusty road we marched, hop yards and bright coloured fields on either side, here and there passing prosperous looking farms and estaminets: what a pleasant change it was from that ruined, dismal jungle we had so recently left! About three or four miles out we came to a village; the main road ran right through it, forming its principal street. On either side small lanes ran out at right angles into the different parts of the village. We received the order to halt, and soon learnt that this was the place where we were to have our ten days' rest. A certain amount of billets had been arranged for, but, as is generally the case, the machine-gun section have to search around for themselves; an advantage really, as they generally find a better crib this way than if somebody else found it for them. As soon as we were "dismissed," I started off on a billet search. The transport officer was again with me on the same quest. We separated, and each searched a different part of the village. The first house I went into was a dismal failure. An old woman of about 84 opened the door about six inches, and was some time before she permitted the aperture to widen sufficiently to allow me to go inside the house. A most dingy, poky sort of a place, so I cleared off to search for something better. As I crossed the farmyard behind, my servant, who had been conducting a search on his own, suddenly appeared round the corner of the large barn at the end of the yard, and came towards me.

"I've found a place over 'ere, Sir, I expect you'll like."

"Where?" I asked.

"This way, Sir!" and he led the way across a field to a gate, which we climbed. We then went down a sort of back lane to the village, and turned in at a small wicket-gate leading to a row of cottages. He led me up to one in the centre, and knocked at the door. A woman opened it, and I told her what I was looking for. She seemed quite keen for us to go there, and asked if there was anyone else to come there with me. I told her the transport officer would be coming there too, and our two servants. She quite agreed to this, and showed me the rooms we could have. They were extremely small, but we decided to have them. "Them" consisted of one bedroom, containing two beds, the size of the room being about fourteen feet by eight, and the front kitchen-sitting-room place, which was used by everybody in the house, and was about twice the size of the bedroom. I went away and found the transport officer, brought him back and showed him the place. He thought it a good spot, so we arranged to fix up there.

Our servants started in to put things right for us, get our baggage there, and so on, whilst I went off to see to billets for the machine-gun section. I had got them a pretty good barn, attached to the farm I first called at, but I wanted to go and see that it was really large enough and suitable when they had all got in and spread themselves. I found that it did suit pretty well. The space was none too large, but I felt sure we wouldn't find a better. There was a good field for all the limbers and horses adjoining, so on the whole it was quite a convenient place. The section had already got to work with their cooking things, and had a fire going out in the field. Those gunners were a very self-contained, happy throng; they all lived together like a family, and were all very keen on their job.

I returned to my cottage to see how things were progressing. My man had unrolled my valise, and put all my things out and about in the bedroom. I took off all my equipment, which I was still wearing, pack, haversacks, revolver, binoculars, map case, etc., and sat down in the kitchen to take stock of the situation. I now saw what the family consisted of; and by airing my feeble French, I found out who they were and what they did. The woman who had come to the door was the wife of a painter and decorator, who had been called up, and was in a French regiment somewhere in Alsace.

Another girl who was there was a friend, and really lived next door with her sister, but owing to overcrowding, due to our servants and some French relatives, she spent most of her time in the house I was in.

The owner of the place was Madame Charlet-Flaw, Christian name Suzette. The other two girls were, respectively, Berthe and Marthe. Ages of all three in the order I have mentioned them were, I should say, twenty-eight, twenty-four, and twenty. The place had, I found, been used as billets before. I discovered this in two ways.

Firstly: On the mantelpiece over the old stove I saw a collection of many kinds of regimental badges, with a quantity of English magazines. Secondly, after I had been talking for some time, Suzette answered my remarks with one of her stock English sentences, picked up from some former lodgers, "And very nice too," a phrase much in vogue at that time.

The transport officer, who had been out seeing about something or other, soon returned, and with him came the regimental doctor, who had got his billets all right, but had come along to see how we were fixed up. A real good chap he was, one of the best. All six of us now sat about in the kitchen and talked over things in general. We were a very cheery group. The transport officer, doctor and myself were all thoroughly in the mood for enjoying this ten days' rest. To live amongst ordinary people again, and see the life of even a village, was refreshing to us. We had a pretty easy afternoon, and all had tea in that kitchen, after which I went out and round to look up my old pals in A company. They had, I found, got hold of the Curé's house, the village parson's rectory, in fact. It was a square, plain-looking house, standing very close to the church, and they all seemed very comfortable there. The Curé himself and his housekeeper only had three rooms reserved for themselves, the rest being handed over to the officers of A company. I stayed round there for a bit, having a talk and a smoke, and we each of us remarked in turn, about every five minutes, what a top-hole thing it was that we had got this ten days' rest.

I then went back to our cottage, where I had a meal with the transport officer, conversing the while with Suzette, Berthe and Marthe. I don't know which I liked the best of these three, they were all so cheery and hospitable. Marthe was the most interesting from the pictorial point of view. She was so gipsy-like to look at: brown-skinned, large dark eyes, exceeding bright, with a sort of sparkling, wild look about her. I called her "La jeune fille farouche" (looked this up first before doing so), and she was always called this afterwards. It means "the young wild girl"; at least I hope it means that. The doctor came back again after dinner, and we all proceeded to fill the air in the small kitchen with songs and tobacco-smoke. The transport officer was a "Corona Corona" expert, and there he would sit with his feet up on the rail at the side of the stove, smoking one of these zeppelins of a cigar, till we all went to bed.

There was an heir to the estate in that cottage—one André, Suzette's son, aged about five. He went to bed early, and slept with wonderful precision and persistence whilst we were making noise enough to wake the Curé a hundred yards away. But, when we went to bed, this little demon saw fit to wake, and continue a series of noises for several hours. He slept in a small cot alongside Suzette's bed, so it was her job, and not mine, to smack his head.

Anyway, we all managed very comfortably and merrily in those billets, and I look back on them very much as an oasis in a six months' desert.

CHAPTER XXVII

GETTING FIT—CARICATURING THE CURÉ—"DIRTY WORK AHEAD"— A PROJECTED ATTACK—UNLOOKED-FOR ORDERS

Military life during our ten days was to consist of getting into good training again in all departments. After long spells of trench life, troops get very much out of strong, efficient marching capabilities, and are also apt to get slack all round. These rests, therefore, come periodically to all at the front, and are, as it were, tonics. If men stayed long enough in trenches, I should say, from my studies in evolution, that their legs would slowly merge into one sort of fin-like tail, and their arms into seal-like flappers. In fact, time would convert them into intelligent sea-lions, and render them completely in harmony with their natural life.

Our tonic began by being taken, one dose after meals, twice daily. In the morning the battalion generally went for a long route march, and in the afternoon practised military training of various kinds in the fields about the village. My whole time was occupied with machine-gun training. Morning and afternoon I and my sections went off out into the country, and selecting a good variegated bit of land proceeded to go through every phase of machine-gun warfare. We practised the use of these weapons in woods, open fields, along hedges, etc. It was an interesting job. We used to decide on some section of ground with an object to be attacked in the distance, and approach it in all kinds of ways. Competitions would follow between the different sections. The days were all bright, warm and sunny, so life and work out in the fields and roads there was quite pleasant. Each evening we assembled in our cheerful billet, and thus our rest went on. My sketching now broke out like a rash. I drew a great many sketches. I joked in pencil for every one, including Suzette, Berthe and Marthe. I am sorry to say I plead guilty to having cast a certain amount of ridicule at the Curé. He was so splendidly austere, and wore such funny clothes, that I couldn't help perpetrating several sketches of him. The disloyalty of his parishioners was very marked in the way they laughed at these drawings, which were pinned up in the row of cottages. Sometimes I would let him off for a day, and then he would come drifting past the window again, with his "Dante" face, surmounted by a large curly, faded black hat, and I gave way to temptation again.

He didn't like soldiers being billeted in his village, so Suzette told me. I think he got this outlook from his rather painful experiences when the Germans were in the same village, prior to being driven north. They had locked him up in his own cellar for four or five days, after removing his best wine, which they drank upstairs. This sort of thing *does* tend towards giving one a bitter outlook. He preached a sermon whilst we were there. I didn't hear it, but was told about it simultaneously by Suzette, Berthe and Marthe, who informed me that it was directed against soldiery in general. His text had apparently been "Do not trust them, gentle ladies." A gross libel. I retaliated immediately by drawing a picture of him, with a girl sitting on each knee, singing "The soldiers are going, hurrah! hurrah!" (tune—"The Campbells are coming").

I'm afraid I was rather a canker in his village.

One day, my dear old friend turned up, the same who accompanied me on leave to England. He didn't know we were having our rest, and searched for me first behind Wulverghem. He there heard where we were, and came on. He was rather a star in a military way, and could, therefore, get hold of a car now and again. I was delighted to see him, as it was possible for me to go into Bailleul with him for the afternoon. We went off and had a real good time at the "Faucon d'Or." We went out for a short drive round in the evening, and then parted. He was obliged to get back to somewhere near Bethune that night. The next day I was just starting off on my machine-gun work when an orderly arrived with a message for me. The Colonel wanted to see me at headquarters. I went along, and arriving at his house found all the company commanders, the second in command, and the Adjutant, already assembled there.

"Dirty work ahead," I thought to myself, and went into the Colonel's room with the others. Enormous maps were produced, and we all stood and listened.

"We are going to make an attack," started the Colonel, so I saw that my conjecture wasn't far wrong. He explained the details to us all there, and pointed out on the maps as many of the geographical features of the forthcoming "show" as he could, after which he told us that, that very afternoon, we were all to go on a motor-bus, that would come for us, down to the allotted site for the "scrap," to have a look at the ground. This was news, if you like: a thunderbolt in the midst of our rural serenity. At two o'clock the bus arrived, and we, the chosen initiated few, rattled off down the main street of the village and away to the scene of operations. Where it was I won't say (cheers from Censor), but it took us about an hour to get there. We left the motor-bus well back, and walked about a couple of miles up roads and communication trenches until we reached a line of trenches we had never seen before. A wonderful set of trenches they were, it seemed to us; beautifully built, not much water about, and nice dug-outs. The Colonel conferred with several authorities who had the matter in hand, and then, pointing out the sector in front which affected us, told us all to study it to the best of our ability. I spent the time with a periscope and a pair of binoculars drinking in the scene. It's difficult to get a good view of the intervening ground between opposing lines of trenches in the day time, when one's only means of doing so is through a periscope.

154

Night is the time for this job, when you can go in front and walk about. This ground which we had come to see was completely flat, and one had to put a periscope pretty high over the parapet to see the sort of thing it was. It was no place to put your head up to have a look. A bullet went smack into the Colonel's periscope and knocked it out of his hand. However, with time and patience, we formed a pretty accurate idea of the appearance of the country opposite. Behind the German trench was the remains of a village, a few of the houses of which were up level with the Boche front line. A great scene of wreckage. Every single house was broken, and in a crumbling state. This was the place we had to take. Other regiments were to take other spots on the landscape on either side, but this particular spot was our objective. I stared long and earnestly at the wrecks in front and the intervening ground. "About a two-hundred yard sprint," I thought to myself. We stayed in the trenches an hour or two, and then all went back to a spot a couple of miles away and had tea, after which we mounted the motor-bus and drove back home to our village. We had got something to think about now all right;—the coming "show" was the feature uppermost in our lives now. Every one keen to get at it, as we all felt sure we could push the Boches out of that place when the time came. We, the initiated few, had to keep our "inside" information to ourselves, and it was supposed to be a dark mystery to the rest of the battalion. But I imagine that anyone who didn't guess what the idea was must have been pretty dense. When a motor-bus comes and takes off a group of officers for the day, and brings them back at night, one would scarcely imagine that they had been to a cricket match, or on the annual outing.

Well, the "tumbril," as we called it, arrived each day for nearly a week, and we drove off gaily to the appointed spot and saturated ourselves in the characteristics of the land we were shortly to attack. In the mornings, before we started, I took the machine-gun sections out into the fields, and by mapping out a similar landscape to the one we were going to attack, I rehearsed the coming tribulation as far as possible. My gunners were a pretty efficient lot, and I was sure they would give a good account of themselves on "der Tag." We practised bolting across a ploughed field, and coming into action, until we could do it in record time. My sergeant and senior corporal were both excellent men.

The whole battalion were now in excellent trim, and ready for anything that came along. A date had been fixed for the "show," and now, day by day, we were rapidly approaching it. It was Friday, I remember, when, as we were all sitting in our billets thinking that we were to leave on Sunday, a fresh thunderbolt arrived. A message was sent round to us all to stand-to and be ready to move off that evening. Before the appointed day! What could be up now? I was full of enthusiasm and curiosity, but was rather hampered by having been inoculated the day before, and was feeling a bit quaint in consequence. However, I pulled myself together, and set about collecting all the machine gunners, guns and accessories. We said good-bye to the fair ones at the billets, and by about five o'clock in the evening the whole battalion, transport and all, was lined up on the main road. Soon we moved off. Why were we going before our time? Where were we going to? Nobody knew except the Colonel, but it was not long before we knew as well.

CHAPTER XXVIII

WE MARCH FOR YPRES—HALT AT LOCRE—A BLEAK CAMP AND MEAGRE FARE—SIGNS OF BATTLE—FIRST VIEW OF YPRES

We marched off in the Bailleul direction, and ere long entered Bailleul. We didn't stop, but went straight on up the road, out of the town, past the Asylum with the baths. It was getting dusk now as we tramped along.

"The road to Locre," I muttered to myself, as I saw the direction we had taken. We were evidently not going to the place we had been rehearsing for.

"Locre? Ah, yes; and what's beyond Locre?" I pulled out my map as we went along. "What's on beyond Locre?" I saw it at a glance now, and had all my suspicions confirmed. The word YPRES stood out in blazing letters from the map. Ypres it was going to be, sure enough.

"It looks like Ypres," I said, turning to my sergeant, who was silently trudging along behind me. He came up level with me, and I showed him the map and the direction we were taking. I was mighty keen to see this famous spot. Stories of famous fights in that great salient were common talk amongst us, and had been for a long time. The wonderful defence of Ypres against the hordes of Germans in the previous October had filled our lines of trenches with pride and superiority, but no wonderment. Every one regarded Ypres as a strenuous spot, but every one secretly

157

wanted to go there and see it for themselves. I felt sure we were now bound for there, or anyway, somewhere not far off. We tramped along in the growing darkness, up the winding dusty road to Locre. When we arrived there it was quite dark. The battalion marched right up into the sort of village square near the church and halted. It was late now, and apparently not necessary for us to proceed further that night. We got orders to get billets for our men. Locre is not a large place, and fitting a whole battalion in is none too easy an undertaking. I was standing about a hundred yards down the road leading from the church, deciding what to do, when I got orders to billet my men in the church. I marched the section into a field, got my sergeant, and went to see what could be done in the church. It was a queer sight, this church; a company of ours had had orders to billet there too, and when I got there the men were already taking off their equipment and making themselves as comfortable as possible under the circumstances, in the main body of the church. The French clergy had for some time granted permission for billeting there; I found this out the next morning, when I saw a party of nuns cleaning it up as much as possible after we had left it. The only part I could see where I could find a rest for my men was the part where the choir sits. I decided on this for our use, and told the sergeant to get the men along, and move the chairs away so as to get a large enough space for them to lie down in and rest.

It was a weird scene, that night in the church. Imagine a very lofty building, and the only light in the place coming from various bits of candles stuck about here and there on the backs of the chairs. All was dark and drear, if you like: a fitting setting for our entry into the Ypres salient. When I had fixed up my section all right, I left the church and went to look about for the place I was supposed to sleep in. It turned out to be a room at the house occupied by the Colonel. I got in just in time to have a bit of a meal before the servants cleared the things away to get ready for the early start the next day. I spent that night in my greatcoat on the stone floor of the room, and not much of a night at that. We were all up and paraded at six, and ready to move off. We soon started and trekked off down the road out of Locre towards Ypres. I noticed a great change in the scenery now. The land was flatter and altogether more uninteresting than the parts we had come from. The weather was fine and hot, which made our march harder for us. We were all strapped up to the eyes with equipment of every description, so that we fully appreciated the short periodic rests when they came. The road got less and less attractive as we went on, added to which a horrible gusty wind was blowing the dust along towards us, too, which made it worse. It was a most cheerless, barren, arid waste through which we were now passing. I wondered why the Belgians hadn't given it away long ago, and thus saved any further dispute on the matter. We were now making for Vlamertinghe, which is a place about half-way between Locre and Ypres, and we all felt sure enough now that Ypres was where we were going; besides, passers-by gave some of us a tip or two, and rumours were current that there was a bit of a bother on in the salient. Still, there was nothing told us definitely, and on we went, up the dusty, uninteresting road. Somewhere about midday we halted alongside an immense grassless field, on which were innumerable wooden huts of the simplest and most unattractive construction. The dust whirled and swirled around them, making the whole place look as uninviting as possible. It was the rottenest and least encouraging camp I have ever seen. I've seen a few monstrosities in the camp line in England, and in France, but this was far and away a champion in repulsion. We halted opposite this place, as I have said, and in a few moments were all marched into the central, baked-mud square, in the midst of the huts. I have since learnt that this camp is no more, so I don't mind mentioning it. We were now dismissed, whereupon we all collared huts for our men and ourselves, and sat down to rest.

We had had a very early and scratch sort of a breakfast, so were rather keen to get at the lunch question. The limbers were the last things to turn up, being in the rear of the battalion, but when they did the cooks soon pulled the necessary things out and proceeded to knock up a meal.

159

I went outside my hut and surveyed the scene whilst they got the lunch ready. It *was* a rotten place. The huts hadn't got any sides to them, but were made by two slopes of wood fixed at the top, and had triangular ends. There were just a few huts built with sides, but not many. Apart from the huts the desert contained nothing except men in war-worn, dirty khaki, and clouds of dust. It reminded me very much of India, as I remembered it from my childhood days. The land all around this mud plain was flat and scrubby, with nothing of interest to look at anywhere. But, yes, there was—just one thing. Away to the north, I could just see the top of the towers of Ypres.

I wondered how long we were going to stay in this Sahara, and turned back into the hut again. Two or three of us were resting on a little scanty straw in that hut, and now, as we guessed that it was about the time when the cooks would have got the lunch ready, we crossed to another larger hut, where a long bare wooden table was laid out for us. With sore eyes and a parched throat I sat down and devoured two chilly sardines, reposing on a water biscuit, drank about a couple of gallons of water, and felt better. There wasn't much conversation at that meal; we were all too busy thinking. Besides, the C.O. was getting messages all the time, and was immersed in the study of a large map, so we thought we had better keep quiet.

Our Colonel was a splendid person, as good a one as any battalion could wish to have. (He's sure to buy a copy of this book after that.) He was with the regiment all through that 1914-15 winter, and is now a Brigadier.

We had made all preparations to stay in the huts at that place for the night, when, at about four o'clock in the afternoon, another message arrived and was handed to the C.O.

He issued his orders. We were to march off at once. Every one was delighted, as the place was unattractive, and what's more, now that we were on the war-path, we wanted to get on with the job, whatever it was.

160

Now we were on the road once more, and marching on towards Ypres. The whole brigade was on the road somewhere, some battalions in front of us and some behind. On we went through the driving dust and dismal scenery, making, I could clearly see, for Ypres. We ticked off the miles at a good steady marching pace, and in course of time turned out of our long, dusty, winding lane on to a wide cobbled main road, leading evidently into the town of Ypres itself, now about two miles ahead. It was a fine sight, looking back down the winding column of men. A long line of sturdy, bronzed men, in dust-covered khaki, tramping over the grey cobbled road, singing and whistling at intervals; the rattling and clicking of the various metallic parts of their equipment forming a kind of low accompaniment to their songs. We halted about a mile out of the city, and all "fell out" on the side of the road, and sat about on heaps of stones or on the bank of the ditch at the road-side. It was easy enough to see now where we were going, and what was up. There was evidently a severe "scrap" on. Parties of battered, dishevelled looking men, belonging to a variety of regiments, were now streaming past down the road—many French-African soldiers amongst them. From these we learnt that a tremendous attack was in progress, but got no details. Their stories received corroboration by the fact that we could see many shells bursting in and around the city of Ypres. These vagrant men were wounded in a degree, inasmuch as most of them had been undergoing some prodigious bombardment and were dazed from shell-shock. They cheered us with the usual exaggerated and harrowing yarns common to such people, and passed on. This was what we had come here for—to participate in this business; not very nice, but we were all "for it," anyway. If we hadn't come here, we would have been attacking at that other place, and this was miles more interesting. If one has ever participated in an affair of arms at Ypres, it gives one a sort of honourable trade-mark for the rest of the war as a member of the accepted successful Matadors of the Flanders Bull-ring.

We sat about at the side of the road for about half an hour, then got the order to fall in again. Stiff and weary, I left my heap of stones, took my place at the head of the section, and prepared for the next act. On we went again down the cobbled road, crossed a complicated mixture of ordinary rails and tram-lines, and struck off up a narrow road to the left, which apparently also ended in the city. It was now evening, the sky was grey and cloudy. Ypres, only half a mile away, now loomed up dark and grey against the sky-line. Shells were falling in the city, with great hollow sounding crashes. We marched on up the road.

CHAPTER XXIX

GETTING NEARER—A LUGUBRIOUS PARTY—STILL NEARER—BLAZING YPRES—ORDERS FOR ATTACK

After about another twenty minutes' march we halted again. Something or other was going on up the road in front, which prevented our moving. We stood about in the lane, and watched the shells bursting in the town. We were able to watch shells bursting closer before we had been there long. With a screeching whistle a shell shot over our heads and exploded in the field on our left. This was the signal, apparently, for shrapnel to start bursting promiscuously about the fields in all directions, which it did.

Altogether the lane was an unwholesome spot to stand about in. We were there some time, wondering when one of the bursts of shrapnel would strike the lane, but none did. Straggling, small groups of Belgian civilians were now passing down the lane, driven out no doubt from some cottage or other that until now they had managed to persist in living in. Mournful little groups would pass, wheeling their total worldly possessions on a barrow.

Suddenly we were moved on again, and as suddenly halted a few yards further on. Without a doubt, strenuous operations and complications were taking place ahead. A few of the officers collected together by a gate at the side of the lane and had a smoke and a chat. "I wonder how much longer we're going to stick about here" some one said. "What about going into that house over there and see if there's a fire?" He indicated a tumbled down cottage of a fair size, which stood nearly opposite us on the far side of the lane. It was almost dark by now, and the wind made it pretty cold work, standing and sitting about in the lane. Four of us crossed the roadway and entered the yard of the cottage. We knocked at the door, and asked if we might come in and sit by the fire for a bit. We asked in French, and found that it was a useless extravagance on our part, as they only spoke Flemish, and what a terrible language that is! These were Flemish people—the real goods; we hadn't struck any before.

They seemed to understand the signs we made; at all events they let us into the place. There was a dairy alongside the house belonging to them, and in here our men were streaming, one after another, paying a few coppers for a drink of milk. The woman serving it out with a ladle into their mess tins was keeping up a flow of comment all the time in Flemish. Nobody except herself understood a word of what she was saying. Hardy people, those dwellers in that cottage. Shrapnel was dropping about here and there in the fields near by, and at any moment might come into the roof of their cottage, or through the flimsy walls.

We four went inside, and into their main room—the kitchen. It was in the same old style which we knew so well. A large square, dark, and dingy room, with one of their popular long stoves sticking out from one wall. Round this stove, drawn up in a wide crescent formation, was a row of chairs with high backs. On each chair sat a man or a woman, dressed in either black or very dark clothes. Nobody spoke, but all were staring into the stove. I wished, momentarily, I had stayed in the lane. It was like breaking in on some weird sect—"Stove Worshippers." One wouldn't have been surprised if, suddenly, one member of the party had removed the lid of the stove and thrown in a "grey powder," or something of the sort. This to be followed by flames leaping high into the air, whilst low-toned monotonous chanting would break out from the assembly. Feast in honour of their god "Shrapnel," who was "angry." I suppose I shouldn't make fun of these people though. It was enough to make them silent

164

and lugubrious, to have all their country and their homes destroyed. We sat around the stove with them, and offered them cigarettes. We talked to each other in English; they sat silently listening and understanding nothing. I am sure they looked upon all armies and soldiers, irrespective of nationality, as a confounded nuisance. I am sure they wished we'd go and fight the matter out somewhere else. And no wonder.

We sat in there for a short time, and stepped out into the road again just in time to hear the order to advance. We hadn't far to go now. It was quite dark as we turned into a very large flat field at the back of Ypres, right close up against the outskirts of the town. Just the field, I felt sure, that a circus would choose, if visiting that neighbourhood.

The battalion spread itself out over the field and came to the conclusion that this was where it would have to stay for the night. It was all very cold and dark now. We sat about on the great field in our greatcoats and waited for the field kitchens and rations to arrive. As we sat there, just at the back of Ypres, we could hear and see the shells bursting in the city in the darkness. The shelling was getting worse, fires were breaking out in the deserted town, and bright yellow flames shot out here and there against the blackened sky. On the arrival of the field kitchens we all managed to get some tea in our mess tins; and the rum ration being issued we were a little more fortified against the cold. We sat for the most part in greatcoats and silence, watching the shelling of Ypres. Suddenly a huge fire broke out in the centre of the town. The sky was a whirling and twisting mass of red and yellow flames, and enormous volumes of black smoke. A truly grand and awful spectacle. The tall ruins of the Cloth Hall and Cathedral were alternately silhouetted or brightly illuminated in the yellow glare of flames. And now it started to rain. Down it came, hard and fast. We huddled together on the cold field and prepared ourselves to expect anything that might come along now. Shells and rain were both falling in the field. I think a few shells, meant for Ypres, had rather overshot the mark and had come into our field in consequence.

I leant up as one of a tripod of three of us, my face towards the burning city. The two others were my old pal, the platoon commander at St. Yvon, and a subaltern of one of the other companies. I sat and watched the flames licking round the Cloth Hall. I remember asking a couple of men in front to shift a bit so that I could get a better view. It poured with rain, and we went sitting on in that horrible field, wondering what the next move was to be.

At about eleven o'clock, an orderly came along the field with a mackintosh ground-sheet over his head, and told me the Colonel wished to see me. "Where is he?" I asked. "In that little cottage place at the far corner of the field, near the road, sir." I rose up and thus spoilt our human tripod. "Where are you going 'B.B.'?" asked my St. Yvon friend. "Colonel's sent for me," I replied. "Well, come back as soon as you can." I left, and never saw him again. He was killed early the next morning; one of the best chaps I ever knew.

I went down the field to the cottage at the corner, and, entering, found all the company commanders, the second in command, the Adjutant and the Colonel. "We shall attack at 4 a.m. to-morrow," he was saying. This was the moment at which I got my *Fragment* idea, "The push, by one who's been pushed!" "We shall attack at dawn!"

The Colonel went on to explain the plans. We stood around in the semi-darkness, the only light being a small candle, whose flame was being blown about by the draught from the broken window.

"We shall move off from here at midnight, or soon after," he concluded, "and go up the road to St. Julien."

We all dispersed to our various commands. I went and got my sergeant and

CHAPTER XXX

RAIN AND MUD—A TRYING MARCH—
IN THE THICK OF IT—A WOUNDED
OFFICER—HEAVY SHELLING—I GET
MY "QUIETUS!"

At a little after midnight we left the field, marching down the road which led towards the Yser Canal and the village of St. Jean. Our transport remained behind in a certain field that had been selected for the purpose. The whole brigade was on the road, our battalion being the last in the long column. The road from the field in which we had been resting to the village of St. Jean passes through the outskirts of Ypres, and crosses the Yser Canal on its way. I couldn't see the details as it was a dark night, and the rain was getting worse as time went on. I knew what had been happening now in the last forty-eight hours, and what we were going to do. The Germans had launched gas in the war for the first time, and, as every one knows now, had by this means succeeded in breaking the line on a wide front to the north of Ypres. The Germans were directing their second great effort against the Salient.

The second battle of Ypres had begun. We were making for the threatened spot, and were going to attack them at four o'clock in the morning.

Ypres, at this period, ought to have been seen to get an accurate realization of what it was like. All other parts of the front faded into a pleasing memory; so it seemed to me as I marched along. I thought of our rest at the village, the billets, the Curé, the bright sunny days of our country life there, and then compared them with this wretched spot we were in now. A ghastly comparison.

We were marching in pouring rain and darkness down a muddy, mangled road, shattered poplar trees sticking up in black streaks on either side. Crash after crash, shells were falling and exploding all around us, and behind the burning city. The road took a turn. We marched for a short time parallel to now distant Ypres. Through the charred skeleton wrecks of houses one caught glimpses of the yellow flames mounting to the sky. We passed over the Yser Canal, dirty, dark and stagnant, reflecting the yellow glow of the flames. On our left was a church and graveyard, both blown to a thousand pieces. Tombstones lying about and sticking up at odd angles all over the torn-up ground. I guided my

What a march! As we proceeded, the road got rougher and narrower: debris of all sorts, and horrible to look upon, lay about on either side. We halted suddenly, and were allowed to "fall out" for a few minutes.

I and my section had drawn up opposite what had once been an estaminet. I entered, and told them all to come in and stay there out of the rain. The roof still had a few tiles left on it, so the place was a little drier than the road outside. The floor was strewn with broken glass, chairs, and bottles. I got hold of a three-legged chair, and by balancing myself against one of the walls, tried to do a bit of a doze. I was precious near tired out now, from want of sleep and a surfeit of marching. I told my sergeant to wake me when the order came along, and then and there slept on that chair for twenty minutes, lulled off by the shrapnel bursting along the road outside. My sergeant woke me. "We are going on again, sir!" "Right oh!" I said, and left my three-legged chair. I shouted to the section to "fall in," and followed on after the battalion up the road once more. After we had covered another horrible half-mile we halted again, but this time no houses were near. How it rained! A perfect deluge. I was wearing a greatcoat, and had all my equipment strapped on over the top.

The men all had macintosh capes. We were all wet through and through, but nobody bothered a rap about that. Anyone trying to find a fresh discomfort for us now, that would make us wince, would have been hard put to it.

People will scarcely credit it, but times like these don't dilute the tenacity or light-heartedness of our soldiers. You can hear a joke on these occasions, and hear the laughter at it too.

In the shattered estaminet we had just left, one of the men went behind the almost unrecognizable bar-counter, and operating an imaginary handle, asked a comrade, "And what's yours, mate?"

Again we got the order to advance, and on we went. We were now nearing the village of Wieltj, about two miles from St. Jean, which we had passed. The ruined church we had seen was at St. Jean.

The road was now perfectly straight, bordered on either side by broken poplar trees, beyond which large flat fields lay under the mysterious darkness. As we went on we could see a faint, red glow ahead. This turned out to be Wieltj. All that was left of it, a smouldering ruin. Here and there the bodies of dead men lay about the road. At intervals I could discern the stiffened shapes of corpses in the ditches which bordered the road. We went through Wieltj without stopping. Passing out at the other side we proceeded up this awful, shell-torn road, towards a slight hill, at the base of which we stopped. Now came my final orders. "Come on at once, follow up the battalion, who, with the brigade, are about to attack."

"Now we're for it," I said to myself, and gave the order to unlimber the guns. One limber had been held up some little way back I found, by getting jammed in a shell-hole in the road. I couldn't wait for it to come up, so sent my sergeant back with some men to get hold of the guns and tackle in it, and follow on as soon as they could. I got out the rest of the things that were there with us and prepared to start on after the battalion. "I'll go to the left, and you'd better go to the right," I shouted to my sergeant. "Here, Smith, let's have your rifle," I said, turning to my servant. I had decided that he had best stay and look after the limbers. I seized his rifle, and slipping on a couple of bandoliers of cartridges, led on up the slight hill, followed by my

It was now just about four o'clock in the morning. A faint light was creeping into the sky. The rain was abating a bit, thank goodness!

We topped the rise, and rushed on down the road as fast as was possible under the circumstances. Now we were in it! Bullets were flying through the air in all directions. Ahead, in the semi-darkness, I could just see the forms of men running out into the fields on either side of the road in extended order, and beyond them a continuous heavy crackling of rifle-fire showed me the main direction of the attack. A few men had gone down already, and no wonder—the air was thick with bullets. The machine-gun officer of one of the other regiments in the brigade was shot right through the head as he went over the brow of the hill. I found one of his machine-gun sections a short time later, and appropriated them for our own use. After we had gone down the road for about two hundred yards I thought that my best plan was to get away over to the left a bit, as the greatest noise seemed to come from there. "Come on, you chaps," I shouted, "we'll cross this field, and get to that hedge over there." We dashed across, intermingled with a crowd of Highlanders, who were also making to the left. Through a cloud of bullets, flying like rice at a wedding, we reached the other side of the field. Only one casualty—one man with a shot in the knee.

Couldn't get a good view of the enemy from the hedge, so I decided to creep along further to the left still, to a spot I saw on the left front of a large farm which stood about two hundred yards behind us. The German machine guns were now busy, and sent sprays of bullets flicking up the ground all round us. Lying behind a slight fold in the ground we saw them whisking through the grass, three or four inches over our heads. We slowly worked our way across to the left, past an old, wide ditch full of stagnant water, and into a shallow gully beyond. Dawn had come now, and in the cold grey light I saw our men out in front of me advancing in short rushes towards a large wood in front. The Germans were firing star shells into the air in pretty large numbers, why, I couldn't make out, as there was quite enough light now to see by. I ordered the section out of the gully, and ran across the open to a bit of old trench I saw in the field. This was the only suitable spot I could see for bringing our guns to bear on the enemy, and assist in the attack. We fixed up a couple of machine guns, and awaited a favourable opportunity. I could see a lot of Germans running along in front of the wood towards one end of it. We laid our aim on the wood, which seemed to me the chief spot to go for. One or two of my men had not managed to get up to the gun position as yet. They were ammunition carriers, and had had a pretty hard job with it. I left the guns to run back and hurry them on. The rifle-fire kept up an incessant rattle the whole time, and now the German gunners started shelling the farm behind us. Shell after shell burst beyond, in front of, and on either side of the farm. Having got up the ammunition, I ran back towards the guns past the farm. In front of me an officer was hurrying along with a message towards a trench which was on the left of our new-found gun position. He ran across the open towards it. When about forty yards from me I saw him throw up his hands and collapse on the ground. I hurried across to him, and lifted his head on to my knee. He couldn't speak and was rapidly turning a deathly pallor. I undid his equipment and the buttons of his tunic as fast as I could, to find out where he had been shot. Right through the chest, I saw. The left side of his shirt, near his heart, was stained deep with blood. A captain in the Canadians, I noticed. The message he had been carrying lay near him. I didn't know quite what to do. I turned in the direction of my gun section without disturbing his head, and called out to them to throw me over a water-bottle. A man named Mills ran across with one, and took charge of the captain, whilst I went through his pockets to try and discover his name. I found it in his pocket-book. His identity disc had apparently been lost.

With the message I ran back to the farm, and, as luck would have it, came across a colonel in the Canadians. I told him about the captain who had been carrying the message, and said if there was a stretcher about I could get him in. All movement in the attack had now ceased, but the rifle and shell fire was on as strong as ever. My corporal was with the two guns, and had orders to fire as soon as an opportunity arose, so I thought my best plan was to see to getting this officer in while there was a chance. I got hold of another subaltern in the farm, and together we ran back with a stretcher to the spot where I had left Mills and the captain. We lifted him on to the stretcher. He seemed a bit better, but his breathing was very difficult. How I managed to hold up that stretcher I don't know; I was just verging on complete exhaustion by this time. I had to take a pause about twenty yards from the farm and lie flat out on the ground for a moment or two to recuperate sufficiently to finish the journey. We got him in and put him down in an outbuilding which had been turned into a temporary dressing station. Shells were crashing into the roof of the farm and exploding round it in great profusion. Every minute one heard the swirling rush overhead, the momentary pause, saw the cloud of red dust, then "Crumph!" That farm was going to be extinguished, I could plainly see. I went along the edge of the dried-up moat at the back, towards my guns. I couldn't stand up any longer. I lay down on the side of the moat for five minutes. Twenty yards away the shells burst round and in the farm, but I didn't care, rest was all I wanted. "What about my sergeant and those other guns?" I thought, as I lay there. I rose, and cut across the open space again to the two guns.

"You know what to do here, Corporal?" I said. "I am going round the farm over to the right to see what's happened to the others."

I left him, and went across towards the farm. As I went I heard the enormous ponderous, gurgling, rotating sound of large shells coming. I looked to my left. Four columns of black smoke and earth shot up a hundred feet into the air, not eighty yards away. Then four mighty reverberating explosions that rent the air. A row of four "Jack Johnsons" had landed not a hundred yards away, right amongst the lines of men, lying out firing in extended order. I went on, and had nearly reached the farm when another four came over and landed fifty yards further up the field towards us.

"They'll have our guns and section," I thought rapidly, and hurried on to find out what had become of my sergeant. The shelling of the farm continued; I ran past it between two explosions and raced along the old gulley we had first come up. Shells have a way of missing a building, and getting something else near by. As I was on the sloping bank of the gully I heard a colossal rushing swish in the air, and then didn't hear the resultant crash . . .

All seemed dull and foggy; a sort of silence, worse than all the shelling, surrounded me. I lay in a filthy stagnant ditch covered with mud and slime from head to foot. I suddenly started to tremble all over. I couldn't grasp where I was. I lay and trembled . . . I had been blown up by a shell.

* * * * *

I lay there some little time, I imagine, with a most peculiar sensation. All fear of shells and explosions had left me. I still heard them dropping about and exploding, but I listened to them and watched them as calmly as one would watch an apple fall off a tree. I couldn't make myself out. Was I all right or all wrong? I tried to get up, and then I knew. The spell was broken. I shook all over, and had to lie still, with tears pouring down my face.

* * * * *

I could see my part in this battle was over.

CHAPTER XXXI

SLOWLY RECOVERING—FIELD HOSPITAL—AMBULANCE TRAIN—BACK IN ENGLAND

How I ever got back I don't know. I remember dragging myself into a cottage, in the garden of which lay a row of dead men. I remember some one giving me a glass of water there, and seeing a terribly mutilated body on the floor being attended to. And, finally, I remember being helped down the Wieltj road by a man into a field dressing station. Here I was labelled and sent immediately down to a hospital about four miles away. Arrived there, I lay out on a bench in a collapsed state, and I remember a cheery doctor injecting something into my wrist. I then lay on a stretcher awaiting further transportation. My good servant Smith somehow discovered my whereabouts, and turned up at this hospital. He sat beside me and gave me a writing-pad to scribble a note on. I scrawled a line to my mother to say I had been knocked out, but was perfectly all right. Smith went back to the battalion, and I lay on the stretcher, partially asleep. Night came on and I went off into a series of agonizing dreams. I awoke with a start. I was being lifted up from the floor on the stretcher. They carried me out. It was bright moonlight, and looking up I saw the moon, a dazzling white against the dark blue sky. The stretcher and I were pushed into an ambulance in which were three other cases beside myself. We were driven off to some station or other. I stared up at the canvas bottom of the stretcher above me, trying to realize it all. Presently we reached the train. Another glimpse of the moon, and I was slid into the ambulance car . . .

In three days I was back in England at a London hospital—"A fragment from France."

Milton Keynes UK
Ingram Content Group UK Ltd.
UKHW012253090224
437600UK00005B/89